MAP ALF K·EBSEN

Whirlpool Farm	Niagara Falls	Casa Loma	Toronto
Beechlands	Thorold	Drumsnab	Toronto
South Landing Craft Centre	Queenston	The McQuay Homestead	Pickering
The Breakenridge House	Niagara-on-the-Lake	Inverlynn	Whitby
The Field House	Niagara-on-the-Lake	The Conant Homestead	Oshawa
The Lyons-Jones House	Niagara-on-the-Lake	Dundurn	Bowmanville
The Stover Homestead	St·Catharines	Terralta Cottage	Port Hope
Rodman Hall	St·Catharines	Penryn	Port Hope
Woodward House	St·Catharines	Strathmore	Cobourg
Lake Lawn	Grimsby	Ravensworth	Cobourg
The Battlefield House	Stoney Creek	The Maples	Grafton
The McNichol Estate	Hamilton	The Whitehouse	Brighton
Fonthill	Hamilton	Springbank	Trenton
The Murton Summer House	Hamilton	The O'Rourke House	Trenton
The Marr Homestead	Ancaster	The Johnston Homestead	Havelock
Hondohnshone (People of the House)	Brantford	The Stewart Homestead	Havelock
Penmarvian	Paris	The Doxsee House	Hastings
Creek Cottage	Ayr	The Willows	Gore's Landing
The Rudy Homestead	Waterloo	The Hutchinson House	Peterborough
The Sonneck House	Kitchener	The Purdy Homestead	Lindsay
The Hespeler Homestead	Hespeler	The Mackenzie Estate	Kirkfield
Bleak House	Guelph Township	The Whiteside Homestead	Little Britain
Sunnyside	Guelph	The Shaw Homestead	Seagrave
Ker-Cavan	Guelph	The Bigelow House	Port Perry
The Bent House	Burlington	The Parr House and General Store	Blackstock
Coleman House	Burlington	Frederick Graham's Homestead	Prince Albert
The Thomas Homestead	Oakville	Cedar Cliff	Brooklin
The Martin Homestead	Milton	The James House	Uxbridge
The Murray Homestead	Halton Hills	The Lowrie Homestead	Scott Township
The Barber Homestead	Georgetown	Tepee	Black River

the drawings of the sixty houses in UNDER THIS ROOF pay tribute to Ontario's diverse heritage

Under This Roof

Under This Roof

FAMILY HOMES OF SOUTHERN ONTARIO

By TERRY BOYLE

WITH COMMENTARY BY PETER J. STOKES

1980
DOUBLEDAY CANADA LIMITED   *Toronto, Ontario*
DOUBLEDAY & COMPANY, INC.   *Garden City, New York*

Library of Congress Catalog Card Number: 79-8925
ISBN: 0-385-15636-7

Printed and bound in the United States of America

Design by Robert Burgess Garbutt

I wish to express my thanks to the following: Thomas Bouckley, Jim Burant, Jean Murray Cole, Patrick Daniel, James A. Dill, John L. Field, Frances Hammerstrom, Imperial Oil, Shirley Langer, Fran MacKay, Allan McGillivray, Rob Mikel, John Morley, Arden Phair, Gery Puley, Mel Robinson, Marg Rowell, Lloyd Saunders, Edith Yeomans, Mrs. Isabel Walker.

Special thanks to the staff of the Robert McLaughlin Gallery: Joan Murray, Director; Grace Turton, Business Administrator; Jane McDonald, Assistant to the Director; Jennifer Watson, Curatorial Assistant-Registrar; Allan Walkinshaw, Curatorial Assistant; Patricia Claxton-Olfield, Librarian; Margaret Jackson, Extension and Education Officer; Alexandra Galbraith, Gallery Assistant; Lucia Raczkowski, typist; Gil Knowler, security.

To the Memory of My Grandmother, Ethel Annie Cole Boyle (1889-1978)

Foreword

How does one choose from the thousands of old houses that dot the early settled southern part of Ontario? To do that, Terry Boyle turned to the people who built or inhabited them, whose expression of need or note they were. From the simplest functional protection from the elements, through man's first struggle to wrest a living from the land, to his arrival at the pinnacle of success, all are represented here, a cross-section of the evolution of the province. Some of the houses are without any pretension, serving only as shelter, others begin to show in their formality a settled attitude to life, possessing a firmness, and not without delight. The author is particularly fascinated with the Victorian, in the middle and later periods, and the Edwardian, when conscious display of position manifests itself in building very expressive of the age of affluence.

This is neither an architectural potpourri nor a selection of personal histories, but rather a testimony to man's affinity to building, to enjoying the art; a demonstration of the simple, the picturesque, and even the grotesque as a personal aspiration. For the hewer of Havelock's 1870 log house must have been as justly proud of his achievement as the builder of the Burlington extravaganza or Sir Henry Pellatt of the castle in the sky created by his architect, E. J. Lennox.

Into the description of every house is woven the story of the people involved with it; thus the buildings themselves are no longer simply monuments to a forgotten past, but vibrant with the life of other generations whence we ourselves came. The individualism of some may make them stand out as "characters," heart-warming with tales of peccadilloes most of us experience to a greater or lesser degree. More's the pity much of our housing today does not offer the same relief.

PETER J. STOKES
September 1979

Preface

As each year passes, a few more glorious old houses disappear; the families who built them have gone forever and with them the early history of this country.

What began as a dream for me has materialized, page by page, into reality. This book is a journey into the past, into an era that displayed vitality and a will to build and to survive. I selected the sixty houses depicted in these pen-and-ink drawings, and I asked thirty artists in various locales to bring their creative talents to this project. Their original artwork forms an exciting exhibition that will travel to eleven cultural centers in Ontario for the public to view.

Under This Roof kindles a warm glow inside me, for I remember the hours I spent listening to my grandmother talk about her early years in Ontario at the turn of the century. This book recaptures something of that past, but I can't help feeling that I've missed something that is unrecoverable.

TERRY BOYLE
Oshawa, Ontario

Contents

Under This Roof

Whirlpool Farm

NIAGARA FALLS

Through a clearing of trees and rising mist stood Whirlpool Farm, gracing a hillside with its appearance. The roar of the Whirlpool Rapids on the Niagara River could be heard from its doorway. English hedgerose and cabbage rose grew along the white picket fence at the front and along the east side of the house; a nine-acre apple orchard prospered across the road, as did another one behind the house. The stone dwelling was spacious, with a wide hallway running from front to back, a dining room and a bedroom to the right, a parlor and a bedroom to the left. All these rooms had fireplaces. The upper floor consisted of three bedrooms.

John Thompson built Whirlpool Farm in 1803 in Stamford (now Niagara Falls), after living eighteen years in a log cabin with his wife, Jeannet. Thompson chose the hillside site for the house to allow for a basement, which faced south toward the river. A kitchen was built in the cellar with a flagstone floor area in front of the fireplace and a spacious bake oven. Behind the house he built several other stone buildings, including a workshop combined with a hog pen and shed attached to the barn, horse stable, sheep house, implement house, and later a cider and sawmill.

After the death of John and Jeannet Thompson their son James assumed the responsibility of Whirlpool Farm. During the War of 1812 he served as an ensign (second lieutenant) in the Regiment of Lincoln Militia, and fought in the Battle of Lundy's Lane.

In 1817 James married Janet Cooper and raised one daughter and seven sons. After Janet Thompson died in 1832 James married Sara Hobson and fathered another two daughters and two sons. All the Thompson children attended school.

Today tourism is a major industry in Niagara Falls, yet the Thompsons experienced it in their day too. Every year people would travel to Whirlpool Farm to view the whirlpool in the Niagara Gorge. Since their property extended from the Niagara Glen to the ravine above the whirlpool, tourists would have to cross the Thompson land to reach it. The Thompsons decided to set out a guest book to record the traffic flow, and in the first year, from June to November, 1845, over fifteen hundred people signed the book. Some had traveled from as far away as Boston, Delaware, Philadelphia, Wyoming, and even England.

Whirlpool Farm remained in the Thompson family until the early 1900s, when Ontario Hydro purchased the property. Eventually the house was torn down and where sheep once grazed, a golfer can now be seen swinging his iron on the Whirlpool Golf Course. Whirlpool Farm is now an apparition, captured in an old photograph, reminding us of what once existed in the wilderness of Niagara.

This stone house was a story and a half high in front with a single story wing on one side. Because of its position at the top of a bank it had an extra story behind. The basement kitchen was reached from the lower level. The main front, protected by a trellis verandah with arches, has five bays and a center door. The roof is a gable of low pitch, with large chimneys placed at the ends. The wing has four openings at the front and a vestibule like a sentry box. The paling fence across the front was a typical enclosure for an early garden.

THOROLD

In 1850 Thorold, Ontario, welcomed its first resident priest, the Reverend Thomas Brock Fuller. A native Canadian, Reverend Fuller was born in Kingston, Ontario, in 1810. His parents died when he was a young child and he was adopted and raised by his aunt Margaret Leeming and her third husband Reverend William Leeming. Thomas Fuller entered the Theological Seminary in Chambly at age nineteen and spent four years there, learning the duties of a missionary by acting as a catechist and Scriptures reader among the Protestant settlers in the area.

A few months after being ordained, he married Cynthia Street, and for about four years he was a traveling missionary until his appointment to Thorold. In 1841, needing a roof over his head, the Reverend Fuller purchased Beechlands, a stone house surrounded by beech trees. It had been built about 1809 on two hundred acres of land by Yeoman Miller, a Kings Guard who had been issued a land grant in 1802.

To the Reverend Fuller a house was the center of all church work and needed to be spacious enough to accommodate visitors and members of the church. He decided to enlarge his house and began construction by removing the west chimney to create a long drawing room in the west half of the ground floor. The fireplace was put on the inside wall against the hall and reconnected to the original stack at the attic level. The east side of the house

was largely preserved. However, the ell was extended and the recess filled in to provide generous domestic quarters, including a large kitchen with bake oven and an internal well. Additional bedrooms and servants' rooms were built above. The old kitchen wing became a dining room lighted by a bay window to the west. Even running water was provided, with a force pump supplying an attic cistern, and the bathroom featured a charming lead-lined bathtub. The interior trim of the house was elaborate downstairs, especially the drawing room with symmetrical profiles and corner blocks with rosettes, and moldings of the 1840s. When the building was completed, Beechlands was one of the finest-looking residences in the area.

To the residents of Thorold, Reverend Fuller was a saviour, even able to stop Sunday traffic on the Welland Canal with his preaching. When he was appointed Rector of St. George's Church in Toronto in 1861, the townspeople regarded his removal as an irreparable loss. And they were proud of the fact that their Reverend Fuller was made the first Bishop of Niagara in 1875. He sold the house to Reverend John MacArthur in 1872, and Beechlands had many owners until the Davis family purchased it in 1941. Mr. and Mrs. William Davis now own the house and property and guard it with great care. Beechlands is more than a historic building to them; it's home.

This stone house, said to have been built around 1809, began as a conventional two-story design with center hall, inside chimneys serving as back-to-back fireplaces, and a kitchen ell extending the west side. But its second owner, Thomas Brock Fuller, embarked on an extensive building program, converting the house to its present form in the 1840s, with a verandah on three sides of the house.

South Landing Craft Centre

QUEENSTON

Sitting on the rise of a hill in Queenston, Ontario, South Landing commands a breathtaking view of the Niagara River, as well as Lewiston and the American shore. Looking rustic in character, the wood frame structure still warms the bank of the river with its presence.

It was May of 1801 when Samuel Streed sold the property to Thomas Dickson. The date of the sixteen-room building is unknown, although an original oil painting of Queenston by C. M. Manly in 1827 shows South Landing on the hill. Mr. Dickson probably built the place since he did not sell the property until November, 1841. By 1883 the Wadsworth family owned and operated the building as an inn, called the Frontier House.

The inn was ideal for accommodating weary travelers. The five-bay front, with the doorway off-center, indicates an unusual plan, for the conventional arrangement was a main entrance to a center hall containing the staircase, with the taproom door at one end. In reconstructing the original plan of this building, the room to the left at the south end contained a fireplace and had an entrance from the side street, and could have been the taproom. Behind was a smaller room that might well have served as a bar. In the middle and to the right of the hall is a large room, now divided by an archway, which originally may have been two rooms: that to the front still has a magnificent ceiling rosette with Greek Revival ornament and a cornice around the room. At the end of the house were several small rooms, perhaps serving as bedroom space. The plan of the second floor is similar to the first except that there are three rooms over the supposed taproom and bar. A ballroom is situated in the middle with small bedrooms extending across the end. Behind the roof's capacious loft space is an ell wing, appearing to be of a later date but possibly replacing an earlier appendage housing a kitchen.

James Wadsworth, the proprietor of the inn at the turn of the century, was notorious for his unlawful activities. During Prohibition he entered into the bootlegging business, storing the liquor in the fieldstone cellar underneath the front verandah and selling it to anyone in the vicinity who was willing to meet his prices. He also ran a profitable operation smuggling immigrants across the river into the United States at fifty dollars a head.

In 1910 the building was sold to Margaret Dressell for three thousand dollars and renamed Riverview Inn. The name was changed in 1947 to South Landing by a later owner. In 1953 Mrs. Rie Bannister, a weaver who had previously operated a weaving shop in Toronto, bought the building, changed the name to South Landing Craft Centre, and for the next twenty-five years people traveled from all over the country to live in this beautiful natural setting and study weaving with her. Her son William, his wife, Carol, and family are now restoring the building to its original state and continuing to operate the business. In spite of looking weather-beaten with its layers of paint baked to a whitish-gray by the sun, South Landing bears a majestic air of tranquility.

This impressive two-story frame building with its double verandah is typical of an early hotel or tavern, and it apparently served as such long ago.

The gable roof of low pitch, the end chimneys, the general proportions, and the disposition of openings are indicative of the first half of the nineteenth century. The clapboard is a characteristic finish. More recently in the building's history, dormers were added and more bedroom space carved out of the loft. The very plain exterior trim, even to the door cases, may be a late change. Window sashes have also been converted to large panes, which rather destroy the scale and historic appearance of the building: upper windows would have had sash of twelve panes over eight, the lower windows possibly twelve over twelve.

The Breakenridge House

On April 30, 1817, John Breakenridge purchased an acre of land and built a magnificent house facing northwest onto Mississauga Street. The builder is unknown, but clearly he was a craftsman, using a typical Georgian plan and building a center door-way with sidelights and a generous fanlight. Inside, the center-hall plan featured the drawing room and the dining room on either side. Upstairs were two large bedrooms, with a small "wig room" over the front hall. The detached kitchen or scullery was located a few feet to the left rear.

The Breakenridge family sold their home in 1824. The house changed ownership until Walter H. Dickson, a prominent man in Niagara, pur-chased it in 1835. It was probably during his ownership that an addition was placed on the rear of the house. The scullery was moved up against the back of the house and a cooking fireplace and bake-oven built into it, with various pantries and work areas added on the main floor. Four smallish bedrooms occupied the second floor of the addition.

In 1902 Major Charles Stanley Herring pur-chased the house, registering it in the name of his wife Marguerite. The major had retired from the British Army after service in India. Although they kept possession of the house for half a century they lived in it only about half that time.

Shortly after World War Two, following the death of Mrs. Herring, the major returned to live in the house. Soon a prospective buyer turned up in the person of Frank Hawley of St. Catharines. Unfortunately, Major Herring was not in a selling mood: "He threw me out," recalls Frank. Within a few years, however, the situation changed. The house was showing the effect of a long period of neglect when he sold to Frank Hawley in 1954. The major had lived in only a couple of rooms and had relied on the dining room fireplace and Quebec heater connected with a stovepipe hole in another chimney. There was a primitive drainage system in the house, but the privy under the pear tree was still in use.

Frank was determined to faithfully restore the old house, but the place required careful study before anything was done. It was discovered that the older part rested on a dry wall only two feet deep, causing it to sink in cold weather so that the hearths were higher than the floors. It had to be jacked up and much work done to provide a proper foundation. While restoration was proceeding, many "finds" were made in and around the house. In the wall of the scullery a sealed-up cupboard was discovered, containing a pewter grog mug made about 1780. A cache of various pieces of sterling silver, some dating from 1731, was found carefully wrapped in oiled paper in the false ceiling of the scullery.

The house itself continues to attract the attention of the discerning traveler. In the winter, and espe-cially at Christmastime when the Hawleys have hung their wreaths on the four front windows and the crystal chandelier in the front hall shines through the fanlight of the door with a rosy glow, the house is a delight to behold.

This handsome two-story house of clapboard, its gable ends finished with a pediment and modillion cornices, is representative of the finer post-War of 1812 rebuilding of Niagara. This is stated to be the second house built in the same block by a Southern lawyer, and by far the most ornate. Two dates have reportedly been seen on sections of the building: one of 1796, which may have been on a piece of salvaged prewar timber; another of 1816, possibly closer to the date of building.

The entrance doorcase has a fine example of the intricate fanlight; the Ionic pilasters and high cornice add considerable dignity to the design. The interior is equally rewarding, not only for its well-preserved complement of trim, but especially for its dining room alcove enclosed by pilasters spirally reeded.

PAUL JOHNS 1979

The Field House

NIAGARA-ON-THE-LAKE

Fleeing from the American Revolution in 1778, George and Rebecca Field sought refuge at Fort Niagara. He was later given Lot 15, a one-hundred acre grant situated on the Niagara River halfway between Niagara and Queenston. He passed the land grant on to his eldest son, Gilbert, who in 1789 married Eleanor Morden and constructed the Field House around the turn of the century.

The Georgian house, made of red brick now weathered to a glowing pink, stood at the top of a gentle rise, facing west toward the river road that wound its way from Niagara to Queenston. The front and rear entrances were centrally placed, connected by a hallway. At the left front was a small room, and behind it was the large "keeping room," in which the family lived, cooked, and ate. On the opposite side of the hallway were two rooms of equal size: the front one was the "best parlor" and the rear one a bedchamber. Both had open fireplaces.

The main staircase rose from the central hallway. Upstairs, on one side were the servants' bedrooms, reached by a narrow back staircase. On the other side were two bedrooms, each with its own fireplace.

In September of 1812, with war declared, Gilbert Field's twenty-year-old son Daniel left with his unit, The Niagara Light Dragoons, to assist General Isaac Brock in the capture of Fort Detroit. Suddenly the Field House was transformed from a family home to a military barracks under the general's orders.

Daniel fought at Queenston Heights and was present at Fort George when the Americans captured it the following spring. And when the Field House was occupied by American troops and used as a barracks and hospital, the family continued to live there rather than risk abandoning the place to the enemy. Peace returned when Niagara was liberated in December, 1813, by British and Canadian forces, and the Field family set about restoring the house and farm. Gilbert Field died a year after the war, leaving the estate to his widow, Eleanor.

The house remained in the family until 1925, when Clayton Field died and his widow sold it and moved out of the community with her two small sons. The house seemed destined for demolition until the late Judge Robert J. Cudney bought it in 1964 and carried out basic repairs and restoration during the next year. In 1968 the Ontario Heritage Foundation bought the Field House from Judge Cudney. The Foundation did not intend to open the house as a museum but advertised it for rent. The first tenants were Mr. and Mrs. John Field, who were kept busy explaining that they were not descendants of the original Field family. Mr. and Mrs. Hudson Stowe now live there.

Those who have resided in the house report that it has an atmosphere in which repose, confidence, and timelessness are mingled.

The Field House is one of the few houses along the Niagara frontier to have survived the ravages of the War of 1812. This two-story brick house, with its five-bay front and center door, typifies the early colonial house of Upper Canada. The sidelights, separated from the front door, are an early feature. Considerable work was done recently to restore certain lost features, such as the many-paned windows, the roof cornices and eaves returns and front porch. The house is reported to have had a steeply pitched roof at one time, much more in keeping with the early date of the house; however, this was burned off long ago and the low-pitched roof substituted. Some of the early detail survives inside but later refurbishing is also evident.

PAUL JOHNS 1976

The Lyons-Jones House

NIAGARA-ON-THE-LAKE

Of the two houses that have been located at 8 Centre Street in Niagara-on-the-Lake, little is known about the first. Records show that on May 6, 1796, James Clark, Sr., received by patent from the Crown a piece of property designated as Lot 193 in the town of Niagara. The house that Clark erected passed on to his son George, but was undoubtedly destroyed when the Americans burned the town as they retired across the river to Fort Niagara in December, 1813.

The story of the present house begins with the next-door neighbors, the Claus family. Colonel Daniel Claus had been Assistant Superintendent of Indian Affairs in New York until the American Revolution. During the war he was forced to flee from the Mohawk Valley along with other United Empire Loyalists. A fine four-acre property in the new town of Niagara was granted to his wife after his death. His son, Colonel William Claus remained to raise his family there and his daughter Catherine married Lieutenant Benjamin Geale, an Irish-born officer of the Forty-First Regiment. During the War of 1812 Lieutenant Geale was wounded and taken prisoner, and as a result of these privations he died in 1821 at age thirty, leaving Catherine to raise their three small children. In 1825 Catherine's father bought Lot 193 from George and Sarah Clark for 125 pounds, and when he died the following year, the property was passed to Catherine.

On June 18, 1833, she married John Lyons in St. Mark's Church. Mr. Lyons, who was the registrar for the counties of Lincoln and Haldimand, had opened a land agency office in the town of Niagara in 1832. In 1836 the ownership of Lot 193 was registered in the name of John Lyons, and it is probable that the present house was built in that year. Though John died in 1844 the name "Lyons" is still associated with the house. Through Catherine's descendants, the house remained in the Geale family until early in this century.

There still exists a pleasant watercolor of the house done by an anonymous artist about 1850. The painting shows the front view of the house, a square, two-story building with a high basement, hipped roof, large shuttered windows, and chimneys in the center of the front and back walls.

The property was bought by Michael Green early in this century and the greens lived in the house until 1963. Mr. and Mrs. W. E. Jones of Toronto bought it in 1965 when Ted Jones was looking for a place in which he could carry on his business as a mechanical engineer. The elegant doorway was hidden by a late Victorian porch that stretched across the front of the house, supporting straggling white wisteria. In order to preserve its character, Joyce and Ted Jones sought the advice of restoration architect Peter Stokes. Both sets of stairs were rebuilt, innumerable layers of wallpaper were removed, and some replastering was necessary. All the windows in the house were redone by craftsmen who had performed similar tasks at Upper Canada Village, and a new picket fence was specially designed for the house. Ted and Joyce Jones moved in on October 1, 1965, and the 1850 watercolor of the house now occupies an honored place in the dining room.

Altogether, the Lyons-Jones house is one that retains the charm and gracious appearance of the Regency period.

This hip-roofed, two-story, roughcast house, epitomizes the late Regency influence on Upper Canada buildings, even to the acceptable deceits of the blind windows, whose closed shutters are set in a recess. These windows, which are on the left, are there to balance the entrance front with the fine doorcase and sidelights and fanlight, and the Venetian window above with a fireplace and chimney right behind. The other façade is notable for the wide openings with sidelights, often referred to as Venetian windows and sometimes called Wyatt windows, after the preference of that architect.

PAUL JOHNS 1978

The Stover Homestead

ST. CATHARINES

This quaint brick house, built in 1845, has aged gracefully with its setting. The four lofty chestnut trees in front and black walnut at the side now tower over this modest abode.

Adam Stover built the house facing St. Paul Street (known earlier as Hamilton Road), for his wife Elizabeth. The interior of the house, heated by wood stoves, contained a spacious living room where the children played on a cozy hand-loomed rug. A wooden couch placed against a wall is where Elizabeth would sit darning clothes and watching the children romp. A tall case clock stood in one corner chiming each hour by; beside it a winding stairway led up to the next floor. The parlor, used for social gatherings, was simply furnished with parlor side tables, rocking chairs, sofa, and a candle stand resting beneath the window. The three low-ceilinged bedrooms were located upstairs.

In 1865 Adam and Jacob Eberhardt, who had married Adam's daughter Phebe, built a back kitchen onto the house. When the addition was completed the two men signed their names on a pane of glass in the kitchen window.

Jacob and Phebe's daughter, Elizabeth, married Clarence Kraft, and after bearing four children, was abandoned by her husband. Unable to cope with her situation, she fled to Kansas City, leaving her children behind for Phebe to raise in the home. Upon her mother's death, Elizabeth returned from the States to greet her grown children and reside in the house again as a member of the family.

The house has changed very little structurally since the day it was built. The trees certainly provide more shelter, and wood stoves are no longer used as a source of heat. Having remained in the family for one hundred and thirty-four years, it now shelters C. Douglas Ayers, a grandson of Elizabeth's, and his wife Mary.

A building in the simple vernacular of the period, the Stover house has some kinship with the Greek Revival designs of the locality in the use of stretcher bond in the brickwork and the vestige of a deep frieze to a former cornice. This story-and-a-half house has a rear lean-to in roughcast. Openings have segmental arches; lower windows are larger, with original sash in six panes over six; the upper gable and wing windows are similarly divided. The front door is still a six-panel version, with fielding and panel molds of the familiar mid-nineteenth-century profile of cyma reversa and sloped fillet. The panel proportions herald later designs, with a long upper panel, but the center panel is small, the lower panel short. However, the low-pitched gable roof has lost the projecting eaves with attendant cornice; the verges are now tight to the walls, and eave returns have been lost, the end chimneys, probably stove stacks, also removed.

L.MAUND/79

AYRES HOME - ST CATHARINES, ONTARIO

Rodman Hall

The strength and dignity of Rodman Hall reflects the character of the man who owned it, Thomas Rodman Merritt.

Thomas Merritt, born in St. Catharines in 1824, was the fourth son of the Honourable William Hamilton Merritt, the man responsible for the building of the Welland Canal. Thomas spent his early years amid the busy scenes of his father's mercantile and political life. He began his own business career in 1844, operating a large general store with a partner. He later branched out by purchasing a flour mill, and, in connection with his mill, he ran an extensive fleet of vessels to carry his produce to the seaboard.

In 1853 he began construction of Rodman Hall. The charm of the house on the hill was reflected in its parklike setting and landscaped grounds. Virtually barren land when construction started, it was soon planted with exotic trees and flowering shrubs to enhance the stylish home. Enchanting walkways bordered sweeping lawns, partially shaded by pine, maple, willow, and black walnut trees. To the east of the house, hidden among birch trees, once stood a summerhouse where the ladies often took tea.

When Rodman Hall was completed, Thomas moved in with his new bride, Mary Benson. The couple lived to celebrate their fiftieth wedding anniversary there in 1903.

Rodman Hall remained in the Merritt family until 1959 when T. R. Merritt, Esq., sold it to the St. Catharines and District Arts Council. The Council renovated it into an Arts Centre, with a new gallery built onto the drawing room. In 1974 the National Museums of Canada announced that it had selected Rodman Hall as a national exhibition center.

Between the foyer and the main hall is a stained-glass partition bearing the Merritt coat of arms. To the left of the hall two drawing rooms were once adorned with Bohemian crystal chandeliers imported from Paris. Now this area is used for art rental and exhibition space. The room now used as a gift shop on the right was originally an oak-panelled dining room. Through the swinging door was the butler's pantry, now the kitchen. The long hallway leading to the right off the mail hall passes the former library, now the tea room. Halfway up the main staircase is an imported stained-glass window, and the room to the right of the stairs on the second floor, now the boardroom, was the upstairs living or morning room. The other rooms on this level were all bedrooms, with the exception of one at the top of the back staircase (now the education office), which was then the billiard room. The third floor had four bedrooms and two storage rooms.

Since Rodman Hall Arts Centre was first established, more than three hundred exhibitions, such as works of James Morrice, David Milne, and Emily Carr, have been open to the public at no charge.

Jacobean Revival might be the closest description for this mid-nineteenth-century mansion. Built in 1853, this house is an elaborate form in stone, with ornamental gables and shafted chimney stacks. The interior contains mantelpieces of Gothic Revival detail, and plasterwork of ceilings is involved with undercut cornices and strapwork in the panels throughout the house. The intricate detail sometimes obtrudes and the building's present function as the local Art Gallery is thereby hampered, neither display nor historic setting faring very well in the ensuing conflict.

Woodward House

ST. CATHARINES

The story of a house is often hidden behind its shutters. The Woodward House has a sad tale to tell.

Built for John Woodward in 1856 by William H. Pay, today this stately, brick house appears lonely, as lonely as its sole occupant, Amy Lalor, a granddaughter of the Woodwards. Amy, who never married, spent the last years of her life nestled inside her home as if her identity had become absorbed by the house.

Eventually the structure became hidden by massive strands of ivy devouring every brick with its foliage and sealing windows from light. The interior trim of pine and the walnut staircase in the front hall faded in the darkness. The ivy even penetrated the interior and Amy retreated to the dining room in the back portion of the house. Night after night she remained sitting by the dining room fireplace warming her chilled body, for the electricity had been shut off in the front part of the house and the only source of heat was the fireplace. Occasionally she would tread down the cellar stairs to the kitchen to prepare a meal. Amy, by now in her eighties and with very little money, would sit glancing around the dining room, occupied with memories of days gone by.

One night in November of 1974 Amy was smoking and set fire to the sofa in the dining room. The flames quickly rose to engulf the entire room. The Fire Department arrived and managed to control the blaze, but by the time they located her, it was too late.

The house went up for sale but remained empty until Eugene and Patricia Trasewick hesitantly walked through the doorway in 1975. Once inside, they were drawn to the house and its intriguing atmosphere. The Trasewicks bought the place and began restoration work. The ivy was torn off the exterior walls and the brickwork sandblasted; the interior received a thorough cleaning and new paint. A new yellow fence replaced the old white picket one. Mr. Trasewick, a lawyer in St. Catharines, turned the basement kitchen into a comfortable office.

Their children, Stephanie and Timothy, now frolic through the halls of the house, bringing new joy to the dwelling that Amy Lalor refused to give up.

When you gaze at the house today, the shutters are open, and you cannot help feeling that Amy would have wanted it this way.

St. Catharines enjoyed prosperity and expansion following the opening of the second Welland Canal in the late 1840's. The building of the period is mainly Greek Revival influence, which is also reflected in place names like Utica, Albany, and Troy. The Woodward House, two-story in the front and one-and-a-half-story in the rear, exemplifies this Greek Revival background with its tall windows, high proportions, Greek doorcase, and parapet end walls.

Lake Lawn

GRIMSBY

In 1710 three brothers, William, Christian, and Johannes Nelles, joined the protestants of northern Germany and immigrated to America, first settling in Duchess County, New York.

A grandson of William's, Henry Nelles, served with the British as a lieutenant in a company of grenadiers in the Revolutionary War. His wife Priscilla and their children were forced to flee to Niagara, as William Canniff, in his book, *Settlement of Upper Canada*, states: "In 1776 there arrived at Fort Niagara, in a starving condition, Mrs. Nelles, Mrs. Secord, Mrs. Young, Mrs. Bowman, with thirty-one children whom the circumstances of rebellion had driven away."

After the war Henry Nelles received a tract of land in Grimsby Township to compensate for the losses he suffered and the services to king and country.

About 1800 his son William, after marrying Margaret Ball of Niagara, built a house near Lake Ontario in Grimsby. William's son, John Adolphus, was left with four small children when his wife died in 1844. He married Helen Sumner a year later and built a magnificent two-story house for his family. They named their new home Lake Lawn because of the pasture stretching from the house to the shores of Lake Ontario.

A prestigious house of eleven rooms, Lake Lawn featured servants' quarters, pantry, winter and summer kitchens, drawing and dining rooms, par-lor, and six bedrooms. Two doors on either side of the pantry allowed a cool breeze to blow through when the servants were ironing there in the summer. Built into the back of the Summer kitchen was a winter privy.

Prior to her marriage to John, Helen kept a diary, and one entry mentions a past love from whom she had recently heard. "I never knew I loved him till now, and O'h shocking to tell him I am engaged to another man . . . He was good and kind and I persuaded myself I loved him and I would never have thought of anyone had I not got a long letter from the favourite youth. He told of his feelings and says time has never changed them. I am convinced now that I loved him then and had I known it was returned I should never have been as I am now, but its too late, my word is given and I shall abide by it. Tomorrow he is to be here to receive my answer and tomorrow I have promised the ever kind one to set a wedding day. O'h my heart will burst."

After John Adolphus Nelles died in 1777, Helen stayed at Lake Lawn until her death in 1896. Their daughter, Florence Louisa Nelles, lived there with her husband, William Manson; later their daughter Florence and her husband, Harold Burnham, owned Lake Lawn. Mary Burnham returned to Lake Lawn in 1947 to stay with her family and now remains there alone.

Lake Lawn is an example of the substantial house of Canada West, a two-story building in soft red local brick, its hip roof of low pitch. Behind is an ell wing, apparently a separate structure, possibly built as an early addition to replace a frame kitchen. A single chimney set forward of the center line and serving a fireplace occurs at each end of the main block, a tall stack at the rear gable of the lower two-story wing. The eaves to the main block have brackets, possibly an addition; there seems to be the remains of a cornice gutter. The front has three openings on each floor; the entrance is a handsome pilastered detail with full transom and sidelights divided into an intricate rectilinear chinoiserie common to the 1840s. Sash-in windows are largely original, in six over six panes of larger glass, slightly smaller sizes occurring in the rear wing. The front is finished in Flemish bond brickwork, the rest of the walls in common bond.

The Battlefield House

STONEY CREEK

James Gage of the 2nd Ulster County Regiment of New York died in action at the battle of forts Clinton and Montgomery in Wyoming on October 6, 1777. Left with two children, James and Elizabeth, Mary Jones Gage claimed and received the equivalent of seven years' half-pay of a private from the government of New York. The widow immigrated with her children to Canada in 1786, settling in Stoney Creek near her family and her husband's brother William Gage. She cleared the land, tilled the soil, and, with the help of her family and neighbors, erected a log cabin. Within the next ten years her son James replaced the cabin with a handsome white frame house known as the Battlefield House. The seven-room house featured a large center hallway; the second floor was one large sleeping loft. In 1830 the Gages changed the sleeping loft into four bedrooms with a center hallway.

In 1796 Elizabeth married Major Westbrook; that same year her brother James married Mary Davis, a member of a Loyalist family who had come from North Carolina. James and his wife continued to reside with Mary Gage. James became a successful merchant, building a general store just southwest of the house which for many years was the only stopping place between Niagara and Ancaster. The area soon became one of the major grain markets in western Canada, due mainly to James Gage's energy and foresight.

James and Mary seldom closed their doors to strangers. On the night of June 5, 1813, the doors of the Gage house opened to the enemy. An invading United States Army of about three thousand men occupied the house and camped in the vicinity. When seven hundred British regulars of the 8th and 49th regiments attacked the American force under cover of darkness, the women and children were locked in the cellar. James Gage was locked in a nearby hut and guarded by a sentry. In the confusion of the battle the sentry ran away and James escaped. He immediately headed for his house, fearing for the safety of his family, and as he crossed the field of fire several bullets punctured his hat. He found his loved ones safe, and when morning broke the vanquished had departed, leaving the house riddled with bullets.

The Gage family left the farm in 1835 and moved to Hamilton, where Mary died six years later at the age of ninety-seven.

The Gage homestead changed ownership several times until Mrs. John Calder, a granddaughter of James Gage, organized a committee of enterprising women in 1899. They formed the Women's Wentworth Historical Society and raised the necessary funds to buy the Gage homestead and the land surrounding it. In 1910 thirteen acres of the original crown grant were purchased, making seventeen and one half acres of parkland open to the public. The parksite and building were taken over by the Niagara Parks Commission in 1962.

It is strange that this historic house survived the Battle of Stoney Creek during the War of 1812; usually such structures are destroyed in the heat of the fight. The house is of the early colonial period, with detail characteristic of that time, essentially of classical origin interpreted in the local idiom or vernacular. The house has been restored to reflect its early history. Later a ballroom was added to the east end and then removed when it first became a public trust earlier in this century. However, the two-story verandah giving a fine prospect of Lake Ontario is one of the original features of the house that remains today.

The McNichol Estate

The year was 1894 when Hiram Herd began construction of a three-story brick house. Wishing a stylish yet contemporary dwelling, he chose late Victorian architecture complete with front verandah extending around the north side and corner tower peering over Hamilton. The interior sported embossed wallpaper, mantelpieces, window shutters of oak, and a spacious drawing room warmed by a glowing fire. When a member of the family or a guest wished to sit and read, he could snuggle up to a cozy fire in the library with a glass of homemade wine from the cellar below. The sitting room and formal dining room were joined, followed by a butler's pantry, kitchen, breakfast room, and doorway leading to the coachhouse. The second floor consisted of six bedrooms, one being the master suite with a fireplace. A tower room used for sewing was situated on the third floor.

After building such a formidable abode, Herd sold it a year later to John Ira Flatt. His daughter Nellie married William James McNichol in 1898 and remained in the house. Dr. McNichol, a well-known physician and surgeon, had studied special surgical work in London, England, and Edinburgh, Scotland. Dr. W. J. McNichol died in 1944 after having practiced medicine in Hamilton for forty-six years. His son, Dr. John Wallace McNichol, a plastic surgeon, remained, working out of the house and caring for his mother.

Dr. John McNichol traveled extensively, lecturing in Mexico and European conferences on conservatism in the treatment of acute injury. The doctor, like his father, spent long hours in his home meeting with patients who arrived at his doorstep for help.

In 1973 Dr. John Wallace McNichol died and his estate was sold in 1976. Adam and Dorothea Weresch became the new owners of the house and are now working on the home with a ten-year restoration plan in mind.

Perhaps the high style of late Victorian building— spilling over into the Edwardian—is this elaborate brick design with high-pitched roofs, many gables, and corner tower like that of a French chateau. This is a natural outgrowth of interest in other French precedents, such as the Second Empire mansard roof. Here an almost complete example shows the elaborate treatment in brick and red sandstone, the gables fitted in with heavily ornamented bargeboards beloved of the 1890s.

Fonthill

HAMILTON

The Greening family first appeared in the annals of history shortly after Columbus discovered the New World in 1492. Christopher Greening, an Englishman who resided in France, was well established in the making of pins in St. Omer. He returned to England in 1563 and his descendants continued in the trade, later branching into the wire industry.

In 1843 Nathaniel Greening founded N. Greening and Sons, Ltd., in England. It was his son Benjamin who retired from the wire industry at fifty-five years of age and immigrated with his wife and family to Canada in 1858.

The crossing was rough, according to a letter written by Benjamin's half-brother Timothy. "Everyone was sick but me," he wrote. Besides sea sickness to contend with, their ship, *The Canadian*, was shipwrecked in the St. Lawrence. Timothy wrote: "The scoundrel pilot ran the steamer at full speed onto a rock scarcely covered with water, within one hundred and fifty yards off Rock Island, on which there is a brilliant lighthouse. The pilot attempted to drown himself when the ship struck."

Arriving in the small city of Hamilton (population 27,500), Timothy prepared to make his way in the new land. Benjamin was content to remain in retirement until an irresistible business opportunity arose. A violent storm destroyed the Great Western Railway bridge at the western entrance to the city. At the time the railway was erecting signals at all the stations on its line and required a considerable amount of wire in the working of them. Benjamin suggested that he could convert the wires from the ruined suspension bridge to suit their purpose. The railway company accepted his idea and commissioned him to carry out the task of making over forty miles of wire strand. As a result of this the B. Greening and Company was formed in 1859. Benjamin's son, Samuel Owen Greening, succeeded as the head of the company after marrying Jane. They lived in Fonthill, since her father had built the place in 1858 and she had grown up there.

The house was named Fonthill because it sat on a hill with a fountain situated to the east of it. Often in the winter Samuel and his family could be seen skating on an ice rink located at the west side of the house. Many evenings were spent in front of the glowing fire, listening to Samuel's stories of his family's past.

After Samuel and Jane died, their family donated Fonthill to the Imperial Order of Daughters of the Empire since their mother had been involved with the IODE most of her life. Now the continuing service work is carried on by the volunteer women who utilize each historical room to further their varied services all over the world.

Fonthill is a large three-story house with a front of three bays, surmounted by a mansard roof with dormers and decorated with iron cresting. It reflects later Victorian changes, possibly to the original 1858 house. It no longer resembles the early form except for its symmetrical façade and perhaps the position of the interior chimneys. The style is of a Second Empire period, which gained tremendous popularity as an urban house design in the last quarter of the nineteenth century. The house stands in the old Duran neighborhood where so many of the fashionable residences were built after 1850.

The Murton Summer House

HAMILTON

In 1791 Augustus Jones named a tongue of land that divides Burlington Bay and Lake Ontario, Long Beach. Appearing as a large sandbar, this strip of land was formed centuries ago by the action of winds and waves depositing silt along a stretch of elevation. Soon marsh plants flourished on the bay margin and eventually trees anchored its shores. The strip was first used as an Indian trail and later by settlers who planted orchards and gardens, gradually building the dirt track. The beach became a naturalist's haven, echoing with the calls of loons, crows, night hawks, and canaries. For the fisherman, hauls of a thousand or more herring were common in the spring, selling at five shillings a hundred in 1854.

Residents of Hamilton and Burlington were naturally attracted to this playground of leisure and sunshine. Many began building stately summer homes and enjoying special excursions and moonlight cruises on Lake Ontario. Some preferred the entertainment provided by the many hotels along the beach. In 1873 a three-story resort named Ocean House was built, offering the summer residences and tourists a dance hall, music salon, bowling alley, billiards parlor, and boat livery by the canal Across the road stood the Royal Hamilton Yacht Club, drawing twenty thousand people to its regattas.

About 1891 Charles Murton of Hamilton built a grand summer home spanning the lakeside. The Murton family was in the coal business, having established the company in 1873. To own a summer home of this stature was very fashionable and many referred to the structure as "the castle."

Perhaps it was the corner tower where stairs led to the four bedrooms on the second floor and two on the third floor which earned it such a name. A twenty-room house with a decorative screened verandah sweeping round it, it featured servants' quarters, butler's pantry, and a breezeway running to the summer kitchen. A bathhouse, used for changing into stylish beach attire, was located in the back yard. For the Murtons, summer evenings were spent strolling the boardwalk or sitting on the verandah conversing about the day's activities.

In time the beach changed from a pleasant scenic playground to a desolate beach polluted by automobile exhaust, hydro towers, and smoke billowing from Hamilton's industry. Fire destroyed many of the summer residences and traditions of an era gone by. The Murton family sold their house in 1945 to the Cahill family. Bud and Betty Cahill still reside in one of the few remaining summer homes that once populated both shores of the strip.

The corner tower, the heavily browed gables to dormers, the small-paned sash in the lunate windows on the second floor, and the spindle-work frieze to the verandah are all trademarks of the late Victorian period around the turn of the century. The house is of the "shingle style" associated with shingle-faced summer residences erected all over the subcontinent in the late nineteenth and early twentieth centuries and particularly in seaside resorts like Bar Harbor, Maine. Wood was used for the interior finish, with paneled wainscots, chevron patterning, or V-joint to walls and ceilings.

The Marr Homestead

Around 1851 Adam Marr of Ancaster built himself a delightful Classic Georgian Colonial house. A cabinet-maker by trade, he constructed his limestone house on the main street, operating his business out of his home. The softening texture of stone and decorative sash mellow into a charming dwelling, simple yet spacious with white pine floorboards.

Marr's property was originally a part of that granted by George III in 1800 to James Wilson, the leader of the United Empire Loyalists who settled in Ancaster as squatters in 1789.

It is no wonder that Adam selected Ancaster to homestead in, for it is a picturesque area. Magnificent ravines cleave the hillside, pleasant little mountain streams cascade into the valley. For a cabinet-maker, the forests offered a boundless supply of lumber. The residents of Ancaster even bottled their fresh water to sell in Hamilton. A Professor George Wilson of Edinburgh had said that the mineral water of Ancaster contained notable medicinal properties and was a useful therapeutic agent.

Adam Marr sold his dwelling in 1875 to James McElroy. The house, like many others, has changed ownership eight times since then. Mary E. McKeon purchased the house in 1977 and opened a delightful bookstore on the first floor. Many customers arriving at the doorstep are curious to see the interior of the house as well as books on the shelves.

This simple three-bay, two-story stone house has a low-pitched gable roof and end chimneys, a mid-nineteenth-century example of the vernacular of classical inspiration. The front is not absolutely symmetrical; the entrance, with the second-floor window aligned with it, is just to the left of center, obviously favoring a slightly larger room on the right. A window at the rear has sash of twelve panes over twelve. Translating this to the openings of the front, those on the ground floor would have been similar, with twenty-four panes, the shorter ones in the second floor with twenty in-sash of twelve panes over eight. The door with transom light above is typical of the period.

Hondohnshone (People of the House)

BRANTFORD

As nature grows and flourishes, so do its people grow in harmony with creation. So it was four thousand years ago with five nations of people in the Mohawk Valley of New York State. Their names were the Cayuga, the great pipe people; the Onondagas, the people of the house; the Oneida, the standing stone people; the Seneca, people of the great mountain; and the Mohawk, people of the flint. Together, they formed a confederacy for the protection and preservation of peace with all things. Their emblem, a tree with large leaves, signified the protection of all people under the tree.

The system of government was one of equal representation of all families in each nation. The eldest woman of each family would select one man of vision who would represent the family for the betterment of all nations in council. Each month the council would meet to discuss the growth and direction of their people. If any man of the council ruled unfairly, he would be dismissed and replaced.

When the colonies decided to sever ties with Britain and war seemed imminent, both the British and the Americans asked the Five Nations to join them. The Confederacy decided to join the British and in turn they received new land by the Grand River near Brantford, Ontario, with the condition that they would be protected by the British and the land would remain theirs forever.

About fourteen thousand people of the confederacy immigrated to the Grand River. They were later joined by the Tuscarora, people of the shirt, from the Carolinas and became the Six Nations.

The Gibson family were a part of the Mohawk tribe. When they arrived on their new land, Gwedamolli (Gibson) built a sturdy longhouse of saplings covered with elm or cedar bark. Their home contained only one room with two openings in the roof to let the light in and the smoke out. A platform covered with skins served as a bed, chair, chesterfield, and wood-box. Gwedamolli's wife would hang her berries, ears of corn, and dried fish from the roof. Privacy was unheard of; everyone shared the interior space and struggled together to survive. The longhouse was a durable home, standing firm against strong winds or heavy rains. The dwelling's sole purpose was to provide shelter.

Lehman Gibson and his family do not live in a longhouse as his forefathers did, but they still remain on the same piece of land. Like his father he teaches his children the way of the warrior in harmony with creation.

More permanent settlements of the original North American inhabitants were simple shelters constructed of easily found local materials. In forested areas, Indians used poles and coniferous tree boughs to fashion communal lodge houses as a protection against the elements. This type of dwelling is a far cry from the sophisticated and considerably costlier European style transported to this continent and designed to satisfy greater demands for comfort and amenity made by less hardy races.

JOHN GACON

Penmarvian

PARIS

In 1674, in Chester, England, Banfield Capron, aged fourteen, stowed away aboard a New England–bound vessel. He landed on the coast near Rhode Island and within six years he had purchased, cleared, and cultivated a large tract of land. When he was thirty-four, life had become too routine and civilized for him, so he trekked farther inland to the Massachusetts frontier where he spent the remainder of his years farming and raising twelve children.

Several generations later, Banfield's restless spirit surfaced again in Hiram Capron, who left home at age twenty to seek his fortune. He began his career as a bookkeeper at a blast furnace near the settlement of Rochester, New York. Six years later he was the principal partner in a foundry he had built on the Canadian shore of Lake Erie near Normandale, Ontario.

While traveling for the foundry he encountered a tract of land near the forks where the Nith River tumbled into the fast-flowing Grand. The land, thickly covered with pine and oak, sloped up sharply to a level oak plain and beyond, into the rolling hills toward Galt. This scene reminded him of his youth spent hunting and fishing in the Green Mountains of New York. He pictured the land for farming and the water power harnessed for mills and industry.

Capron purchased the land in 1829 and moved his young family to the new area. After he successfully raised money to improve Governor's Road (surveyed and built in 1793) and to build a bridge across the Grand River, settlers began to come.

His land was surveyed into streets and lots, the lots being offered free to settlers. A dam was built with raceways and gristing-grinding mills, thus bringing more enterprising business people and hardworking settlers to the new village of Paris. The villagers called Capron "King."

The house he built was made of square hewn stone in a simplified Classical Revival design; it crowned the hill overlooking Paris, commanding his favorite view of the Grand River below as it wound south to the wooded banks at the forks. The house was large enough to accommodate his family of six children, yet sedate and restrained.

The second owner of Capron's house was John Penman of the Paris textile mills who gave it the name "Penmarvian." During his ownership Victoriana was influential and he attempted to embellish the house into a castle with conical tower, gables, and blocky pink columns. After the home was willed in 1939 to the Presbyterian Church it was used as a retirement home for ministers. In the 1960s and '70s it was available for rent as a family home to prevent it from reaching abandoned status. In 1977 the owner of a construction firm bought Penmarvian and began extensive renovations to restore it.

The original beauty of King Capron's home died with him in 1872 and his six children are gone, leaving no descendants. However, the children's names remain alive as street names in Paris— Emily, William, Mary, Banfield, Jane, and Charlotte.

Penmarvian was originally the home of Hiram Capron, who brought with him from upstate New York such builders as Levi Boughton, experienced in the cobblestone tradition. Penmarvian, however, is more conventionally of cut stone. The classical formality of the original design has been completely supplanted by the reinterpretation of a slightly chateau-like façade, rather evocative of Vanderbilt mansions, and possibly inspired by like tastes, namely the expression of the self-made man, the textile manufacturer, John Penman. It is the composite that is perhaps of greater significance, although the loss of Capron's counterpart to the fine cobblestone buildings of the town may well be regretted.

Creek Cottage

AYR

The hauntings of Creek Cottage are spine-tingling, yet partially explained as one unravels the story of the Wyllie family. When Robert Wyllie and his wife arrived in Ayr, Ontario, in the 1840s from England, they built a quaint cottage by the shore of the Ninth River. Their home reflected an air of simplicity and timelessness. Built on a flood plain, it was protected by a dike-like foundation to survive yearly floods that threatened to sweep it away.

Robert soon established himself as Ayr's first postmaster and became a highly respected man in the community. However, the Wyllies had a skeleton locked away in their closet. Apparently Mrs. Wyllie's sister had been a mistress to the poet Robert Burns and during their relationship they had exchanged numerous love letters. After the death of her sister, Sarah had brought the letters to Canada with her and stored them away somewhere in Creek Cottage. Not wishing to leave her letters behind, Sarah's sister would return in a ghostlike state to search for them.

When Devona and Phil McLorn purchased the house in 1976, they were unaware of this story until they experienced two separate visitations of the ghost of Creek Cottage. The McLorns had just comfortably settled into their new environment when one winter night at four in the morning they were suddenly awakened by a knocking at the front door. Phil ran to the door, but when he opened it, no one was there. Since most people use the side entrance of the house, the snow is never removed from the front walkway and a new snowfall had covered earlier footprints. But when Phil looked for new footprints in the snow he could find none. Whoever the visitor was had not walked up to the front door. Somewhat startled and confused, Phil retired to bed, unable to explain the knockings at the door. The next day Phil and Devona chatted about the strange occurrence and then quickly dismissed it from their minds until a few nights later. Once again in the middle of the night they were both awakened by the creaking of the trapdoor in the kitchen as it was lifted up. Then they heard a loud slam as the trapdoor closed. Devona quickly rose out of bed and cautiously moved toward the kitchen. When she reached the kitchen doorway, no one was to be seen. A thorough search of the house revealed nothing. Once again their visitor had left without a trace. Unable to explain this second visit, the McLorns asked the previous owners of the house if similar things had ever occurred. The answer was yes. Since then the ghost of Creek Cottage has left the McLorns in peace, leaving us to wonder if Sarah's sister found the letters she so dearly cherished.

The epitome of the Regency cottage of Upper Canada and Canada West, this house is a single-story structure with capacious loft in the space of the hip roof forming a low pyramid crowning the building. The loft is lighted by the two dormers to the front. The front, of five bays with center entrance, overlooks the river. The protecting verandah with lattice balustrade and bowed roof is typical of such buildings. It probably had end chimneys originally for stove heating. This house is reminiscent of many others in the area and elsewhere in southern Ontario, some of brick and stone and often referred to as the "Ontario cottage."

MCLORN

The Rudy Homestead

WATERLOO

In the countryside of Waterloo stands an impressive, eleven-room home built of granite fieldstones of varying shapes and colors. The five-bay house, sheltered by a tin roof painted green, was built in 1847 by Daniel Rudy. A belfry was added to the center roof for the women to use when calling the men in from the fields for supper. The stonework underneath the front verandah was stuccoed over and marked out to represent blocks. The main support beam in the basement is ax-hewn. The interior walls are painted plaster over granite and the floorboards are pine.

The center hallway has a stairway of oak dating from around 1890. Many of the interior doors are six-paneled with older-styled thumb latches. Upstairs are two bedrooms with baseboards and window trim of very plain pine. A door leads from the second-floor hallway to a small balcony over-

looking the rolling hills of Waterloo. Here on the wall you can see a semicircular stone inscribed: *Daniel Rudy, 1847.*

About 1860 a back wing, with board and batten washhouse and woodshed attached, was added to the house. The cellar under this wing had a dumb-waiter and an old wood-burning schnitz (apple) drier.

Daniel Rudy sold his homestead and two hundred and twenty-four acres in 1866 to Christian Snyder and his family. The land remained in the Snyder family until 1976, when Dorothy Snyder kept the house but sold the land for redevelopment.

Waterloo's urbanization has quickly engulfed this farming district. The fields across from the homestead that once grew corn now support planted rows of urban housing.

The Rudy home was built in 1847. The orientation, the arrangement, the simple bold massing, and the formality of this building in a vernacular of classical inspiration proclaim this to be a Waterloo County house of the Mennonite tradition. It has a two-story, five-bay front, with windows having sash of twelve panes over eight; the gable ends are ornamented with eaves returns. One end chimney for a stove flue survives, the other apparently in the original serving at least a basement fireplace in the west end. The stonework is common in the area, the masonry of split fieldstone, a colorful mixture of granite, with large stones set to form the corners and an infilling of smaller pieces much augmented by generous mortar joints struck neatly with lines to give more regularity to the work. The lintels are in a flat arch form, but of timber. The verandah columns are a simplified version of the Tuscan order, rather Germanic in feeling, although these may be a later replacement.

The Sonneck House

KITCHENER

The name Breithaupt is prominently inscribed in the annals of Kitchener history. Liborius Breithaupt, as were his father, grandfather, and great-grandfather, was a tanner in Allendorf an der Werra, Kurhessen, Germany. Breaking tradition, Liborius left Germany in 1842 to begin a new life in America. Scouting the countryside for a suitable location to begin a tannery business, he chose Buffalo, New York, and after returning briefly to Germany for his family, in 1844 he established a tannery under the name L. Breithaupt and Company. Upon his death his son Louis Breithaupt succeeded him and formed a partnership with Jacob F. Schoelkopf. When their partnership dissolved in 1861, Louis left Buffalo and settled in Berlin (Kitchener) to build another tannery. Berlin was not unfamiliar to Louis, for he had made several business trips there in the past.

Breithaupt took a very active part in fostering the growth of Berlin. A member of the town council as well as a businessman, he served his constituents well. Shortly after his business was built, fire leveled the buildings in 1867 and again in 1870. Breithaupt rebuilt his empire again with unrelenting determination.

During this time his son Louis Jacob began his apprenticeship in the tannery and office. Spending four years on the road as a commercial salesman for the firm, he slowly advanced step by step to become manager, at age twenty-five. He, too, was actively involved in anything that concerned the welfare of the community.

About 1875 Louis built a handsome mid-Victorian house on a corner lot on Queen Street. He named the home "Sonneck," which means "sunny corner" in German. Originally the home featured a main staircase, reception room, drawing room, and formal dining room. Each room had a spacious grace and a comfortable aura, which the elegant decorating reflected. Trees planted on the grounds shaded the outskirts of the property, leaving the house exposed to full sunlight.

Louis Jacob followed in his father's footsteps, serving as mayor of Kitchener for a time and eventually as president of the Breithaupt Leather Company Limited. His son, Louis Orville Breithaupt, later served as lieutenant-governor of Ontario.

When Mr. and Mrs. Jack Smith purchased Sonneck house in 1963, the home had been renovated into a triplex during World War Two and no longer retained its original appearance. The original interior plan was completely destroyed.

The principal influence evident in this mid-Victorian house is the Italianate with the low-pitched roofs and bracketed eaves combined with an elaborate outline. The tower feature is absent, and bay windows have become part of the composition. An original chimney near the center of the house still has an elaborate pilastered stack. The entrance porch is a later improvement in part, and a previous owner has given unwarranted emphasis to the windows by subdividing the sash from the original two panes over two, a process sometimes referred to in preservation circles as "earlying up." But the bay windows are intact, with complex fretwork at the eaves and a cut-out pattern to the infilling of the edge panel characteristic of the incised wood decoration of the period. Regrettably, some of the original joinery, such as the main staircase, has disappeared in the building's conversion to a triplex.

MCLORN

The Hespeler Homestead

HESPELER

Few settlers in southern Ontario built their homes to accommodate a love of horses as Jacob Hespeler did. Arriving in New Hope (later named Hespeler) about 1840, Jacob built a massive two-story limestone dwelling on top of Guelph Road Hill in 1867. The house, surrounded by lovely gardens, looked out across the Speed River and the tiny settlement. To the east of the house was an archway leading into the stables. The coachman who fed and groomed the horses resided above the stables. The main part of the house was decorated with high ceilings in keeping with the aspirations of a successful mid-nineteenth-century entrepreneur. The drawing room featured interior box shutters on the windows and a stock marble mantelpiece. Most rooms expressed formality and spaciousness with grand archways and panels carved with grapevine design.

Jacob Hespeler was a man with a genius for business organization. He bought a grist mill and purchased a large tract of property that gave him control of the west bank of the Speed River. A German immigrant, he developed and settled an area of land known as Pine Bush with German immigrants and later added a flour mill, sawmill,

distillery, and woolen mill to his enterprises. A Lutheran noted for his generosity and principles of good living, he gave financial aid to the Roman Catholics of the settlement to build their first church. When the Great Western Railway was being constructed through Galt, Preston, Hespeler, and Guelph, Hespeler took advantage of the situation and had the settlement incorporated as a village. At that time one hundred freeholders and householders signed a petition to be incorporated under a new name, Hespeler, in honor of the man who had contributed to the prosperity of the settlement.

Leaving Hespeler in the early 1870s, he journeyed to California and entered the cattle business. He died in March, 1881, shortly after his return, and was buried in the Hespeler Cemetery.

His handsome estate has seen many changes and tenants. The grounds have been greatly reduced in size, with a playing field on one side and a new factory below the house. The house is now an apartment building and occasionally the tenants sit outside underneath a charming lattice summerhouse with a pagoda roof built at the beginning of the century.

The original appearance of this handsome stone structure is hard to imagine because many exterior additions and internal changes have occurred in its long history from the home of a wealthy and influential local industrialist to an apartment building. It comprises a main block with generous windows to the street, probably with twin double-hung windows, or Venetian windows, with a center light flanked by half-width sidelights, but filled in with plate glass and a stained glass transom for a turn-of-the-century improvement. The doorcase is a characteristic design with sidelights and transom. Behind is a wing, also of two stories, like the front and rear blocks, but with curious round-arched windows to the upper story on both sides and in front an arcaded lower section, apparently an addition and now filled in. Behind is a high, narrow block, still with original sash in some of the windows that have six panes of the attenuated vertical proportion common to the Greek Revival and Italianate.

Bleak House

GUELPH TOWNSHIP

In 1827, the year Guelph was founded, an Englishman tramped through the forests searching for a space to settle. John Neeve located a place near Marden in what is now Guelph Township.

Since the forests were being cleared for a new road, it was an easy matter to select choice cedar logs for building. Choosing a knoll as an ideal location, he constructed a large log house, measuring thirty by forty feet, with three gable windows. On the first floor there were two spacious rooms and a winter kitchen, with four bedrooms on the second. The house changed ownership twice until William Fox Davis purchased it and persuaded his promised wife to come out from England to live there.

Unfortunately, she was not impressed with the new country and soon returned to her homeland. Discouraged and heartbroken, Davis sold the farm to a Mr. Marsh. His wife, a great reader of Charles Dickens's books, named the house Bleak House, the name it still bears today.

John Card bought Bleak House in 1827, and one hundred and one years later his great-grand daughter Jean and her husband, John A. Reilly, inherited the farm. John and Jean raised their two daughters, Anne and Sheila, in this beautiful environment.

A grove of spruce trees growing along the road sheltered the house from the wind; a towering tree graced either side of the front entrance. Purple and white lilac trees encompassed the smokehouse, behind the log house, with fragrant scents. A fieldstone fence marked the curves and bends of the land in front of the house.

During the Depression, the Reillys managed to survive without losing their home. When logs at the side of the house needed to be replaced and little money was available, they rebuilt part of the side wall with fieldstone.

John Reilly died in 1969, and Jean, with her daughter, Anne, continued to farm the land until 1975. Today, almost everything remains untouched. Recently the smokehouse was torn down but the homestead remains, standing firm, rooted to the generations it has sheltered.

Sequestered behind majestic spruces planted almost a century ago this commodious log house would be one of the earliest permanent dwellings in the area, for its date of building corresponds with the founding of Guelph. The logs are squared timbers, dovetailed at the corners, those over the windows stretching the forty-foot length and thirty-foot depth of the building. These dimensions and its story-and-a-half height give the house the effect of hugging the ground (emphasized by its timber walls exposed to the outside weathered from a silver to a dark gray). The narrow verandah that once encircled the house has been removed. The roof is a medium pitch with high gables framed in and finished with vertical board and batten, the north gable with smaller windows of two six-paned sash; those on the south are two twelve-paned sash like some of the ground-floor windows.

Sunnyside

GUELPH

In lighthouses along the coastline of Scotland, William Kennedy acquired a myriad of memories which he later incorporated into the building of Sunnyside.

In 1814 Sir Walter Scott, the famous novelist, and Robert Stevenson, an engineer, sailed past the Bell-Rock Lighthouse then under construction. Sir Walter expressed an interest in the view from the highest peak of the evolving structure. The two beached their craft and approached William Kennedy, who was the superintendent of construction, on the possibility of venturing to the top for a look. The construction basket, activated by rope and pulley, carried Scott and Kennedy to the top and the brief encounter remained indelibly fixed in the builder's mind for many years. Later, Kennedy would carve a bas-relief sculptural interpretation of "Abbotsford," the Scottish residence of Sir Walter Scott, in his own home as a gesture of his admiration for the man.

Arriving in Canada in 1833, Kennedy first worked on the early construction of the Kingston Penitentiary; then he purchased a farm in Nichol Township, north of Guelph, Ontario, and built himself a log house. Using upright logs, in the French manner, for his house, he subsequently earned the nickname "Upright Kennedy." His nickname changed to "Yankee" following a stay in Philadelphia from 1839 to 1847. His son, David Johnston Kennedy remained in Philadelphia to combine his talents as an artist and a skilled stonecutter like his father. His ability as an artist led to "the most comprehensive and single-handed graphic record of any American city," according to *David Johnston Kennedy, A Painter of Guelph*, by Judith M. Nasby. The Historical Society of Philadelphia now possesses seven hundred and fifty of his pencil drawings and watercolors of the city's architecture.

The construction of Sunnyside began in 1853. It was built of Guelph limestone, and one of its major features is the unique carved stone portico facing the River. The living room also contains an unusual carved limestone fireplace, which Kennedy devised using a collection of classic and Gothic details. A short Corinthian column, carved by William in 1848, stood on the grounds supporting an old sundial that had previously sat on the stump of the first tree cut by John Galt, the founder of Guelph.

On nearing the completion of his project, William Kennedy wrote a letter to his son dated January 7, 1855. In it he described his work on the house to date and enclosed plans and elevations of its design, and instructed his son on the completion of the portico should he die suddenly (he was seventy-two at the time), but he was able to add the unique and intricate finishing details.

After completing his house, William gave it to his youngest daughter, Jeanie. She and her husband, Charles Davidson, a Guelph businessman, passed the home onto their family. Sunnyside remained in the possession of the Davidson family until 1977.

Sunnyside is a three-bay, two-story, hipped-roof house built of local limestone. The form is conventional for the period, the end chimneys completing the formal composition. The house is remarkable for the portico on the garden front facing the Speed River, in Guelph. This is a highly skilled and deeply personal work of the builder and owner of the house, William Kennedy, a master mason who was carving this work at age seventy-one. The Ionic pillars carry an entablature crowned by a curious high parapet rather reminiscent of the Greek Revival and perhaps inspired by works seen long before in the Athens of the North, namely Edinburgh.

COULING '79

Ker-Cavan

GUELPH

Reverend Arthur Palmer was founder of many Anglican parishes in the Guelph area. Born in Galway, Ireland, in 1807, he came to Canada in 1832 to become the first rector of St. George's Church in Guelph. He remained there some forty-two years and acquired extensive property, including an impressive seventy-acre estate on the hillside facing the town, rising above the east bank of the Speed River. Palmer purchased the estate in 1846 and, according to local tradition rather than official documentation, elicited the services of Sir Charles Barry, a famous British architect, for the design of his new home (Sir Charles Barry planned the Houses of Parliament between 1840 and 1865.) This house in Guelph is the only architecture attributed to Barry in North America. Construction was probably supervised by a former student of Barry, architect Frederick Rastrick.

A large limestone house was built on the brow of the hill and named "Tyrcatheleen" or "Tycathe-leen." Local legend has it that if Archdeacon Palmer had been nominated as the first bishop of the Hamilton diocese, he would have given the property to the Anglican church.

Palmer retired to his native Ireland in 1874 and the house was sold to Alex B. Petrie, a local druggist and manufacturer. In 1926 it was purchased by Henry B. Higinbotham, an insurance executive born in Guelph and an extensively traveled man. In the next two years Higinbotham enlarged the structure that came to be known as Ker-Cavan. After his death the house was owned by Brigadier Kenneth S. Torrance. His sister, Anna, became the wife of Henry Higinbotham's brother, John.

In the 1960s Ker-Cavan became Greenhill Nursing Home and the large coachhouse is now an annex for the nursing home. About five acres of the original estate surround the house with vast lawns and many great trees. some over one hundred and twenty years of age.

Ker-Cavan is a Gothic Revival house of stone in the Tudor manner. The house was enlarged earlier in this century (1926-28) by the English architect H. R. Coales. The house has now a greater symmetry than the picturesque composition of the original. The stonework of the original is a finely executed ashlar, the cut stone of the additions carefully matched with salvaged material from an 1850 house, "Rosehurst." The house is an impressive structure and retains substantial grounds, as well as a large coachhouse of half-timbered design.

COULING

The Bent House

BURLINGTON

When James Bent built this house in 1885, he created a masterpiece of originality. The small six-room house located on Ontario Street in Burlington even had two roofs, likely for double protection. Bent constructed one roof over the building, then plastered over it and built another one on top. A verandah swept around the west side of the house with a back kitchen and woodshed shaded by a maple tree in the back. The interior plan featured a spacious parlor with a fireplace, living room, and winter kitchen. An oak staircase led to the two bedrooms and sewing room on the second floor. The center chimney leading down to the parlor is quite picturesque from the outside, with twin shafts having highly ornamental caps. Being a master builder, Bent built the house as an investment and sold it in 1888 for $1,575.

Joseph and Hannah Alton purchased the house in 1894 for $1,800. Born in Burlington, Joseph was raised on the Alton farm located north of the Queen Elizabeth Highway and west of Appleby Line. When he made out his will in 1898, Joseph made sure his wife would be provided for. He wrote: "I further will that my son Theophilis shall supply his mother, my wife, the said Hannah Alton, with one cow and feed therefore, if she shall so desire, also all the wood cut and split, as she shall require during her natural life." The house remained in the Alton family until 1904, and then passed from one owner to the next. In time the back kitchen and woodshed disappeared and side verandah was enclosed. In 1955 Mearle and Florence Middletown drove by the house and stopped. It was for sale and they bought it. That was twenty-four years ago and although the front part of the house is now an apartment, they still reside there.

The history of the builders of many houses, or the people who first lived in them, has disappeared. Families die out, and if they did not play a significant role in community affairs little has been recorded. Thus James Bent remains virtually unknown except for the house he built over ninety-four years ago.

This curiously finished small house looks a little like a carpenter's whimsy. It is not only strange in its detail but original in its design. Basically the house comprises a center block a story and a half high with a gable to the street and lean-to wings on either side. But this form is hard to recognize behind the tour de force of the front. The entrance is set back to form a recess, or umbrage. This is now filled in with glazing so that the narrow roof projecting as further protection to the porch and steps rather loses its effect. In the gable is an odd shallow triangular parapet, intricately ornamented along the top with carved and indented dogtooth ornament of two kinds in bands. The center feature, at the crest of the gable is a finial through an open half-circle like a rainbow.

Ken Montgomery
79

Coleman House

Burlington has one of the most unique villas, possessing Victorian character, in southern Ontario. The Coleman house, built by Mr. A. B. Coleman in 1893, is commonly known as the Gingerbread House. It displays eclectic detail that is not only beguiling but breathtaking. Rising to a splendid two-and-a-half stories in front, the lower section of the house is of wood clapboard ascending to numerous styles of decorative wood shingles, looking almost like fish scales.

Coleman was an energetic and progressive general contractor and lumber builder in Burlington. He began business as a contractor at the age of eighteen and later owned a planing mill on Ontario Street, west of his estate.

The interior items of interest in the Coleman house are numerous. The elaborately worked fireplace and mantel are complemented by a roundheaded, stained-glass window appearing above in the brick chimney. The stained-glass doors and decorative components of wood and plaster in the ceilings are sumptuously constructed.

In 1899 the *Gazette* newspaper ran an advertisement stating: "Mr. A. B. Coleman has sold his beautiful residence on Ontario Street opposite St. Luke's Church to Dr. Metherell, of Hamilton." The doctor, who administered to the local townspeople, would leave each morning from the carriage house in a buggy to make his house calls.

Dr. Metherell sold the house to William Ford in 1912. Mr. Ford added a rear kitchen that year and renovated the interior in 1940 to accommodate two apartments. Thomas and Ivy Thompson, who had rented a room from Fort in 1928, never allowed their eyes to stray from the house and when Mr. Ford decided to sell, Thomas Thompson was there to buy.

The villa fantastique, Victorian wizardry in wood, a sight for the sorest eyes, whimsical exuberance in the extreme—you can never fault this example of the Gay Nineties for mediocrity.

The house is a complicated shape of projecting bays and wings, gables and porches, bays of rectangular and octagonal shape, porches to the entrances and from bedrooms as well as from the attic. Windows, many partly filled with stained glass, some with slightly Art Nouveau designs, are of various shapes of half-moons, quarter-moons, plus many plainer sash types, the outer edges divided into a surround of smaller panes.

Surface treatment features a great variety of ornamental finishes, including pattern shingling, vertical board and batten, and ribbed horizontal siding. The entrance porch, with groups of slender columns supporting it, has a pediment front sporting a center rosette, corner fans, dentils, and brackets to cornices, then a form of spindle work below.

Ken Montgomery '79

The Thomas Homestead

OAKVILLE

After the death of his mother young Merrick Thomas left his brothers and sisters in Queenston to make his own way. He eventually settled in Saltfleet, Ontario, living with his employer, William Kent, who operated a general store, saltworks, and sawmill as well as several Lake Ontario vessels. Merrick held a number of jobs from sawyer, sailor, and clerk to the final position of general manager. Leaving Kent, he went to Tulson, Ontario, and became general manager for Colonel William Chisholm, who was engaged in a very extensive mercantile and lumber business.

In 1827 Colonel Chisholm purchased nine hundred and sixty acres of uncleared land at the mouth of Sixteen Mile Creek, now known as Oakville. He appointed Thomas to be in charge of constructing a new settlement. Merrick Thomas became the driving force in this enterprise, having the forests cleared, the area surveyed, and buildings erected. He oversaw the construction of the harbor and the shipyard, along with the building of saw- and grist mills.

In 1827 Merrick married Esther Silverthorn of a Loyalist family from New Jersey and sister of William Chisholm. They raised seven children, one of whom, Charles William, became a shipbuilder at age eighteen. Charles would build the schooner *Crescent,* which was lost with all hands on board in Lake Ontario.

In 1829 Merrick leased two hundred acres of Crown Reserve on Lot 17, Concession 3, paying a yearly rental of ten shillings or three bushels of good, sweet, clean mercantile wheat. For his house he laid a foundation of fieldstones, leaving several pine stumps within the rectangle of the foundation. The house, made of white pine timbers, was built on top. Pine logs were drawn to the sawmill and cut into boards for sheathing, flooring and interior trim. At one end of the front verandah was a window staircase that led to the bedrooms on the second floor. The first floor contained only a large room with a fieldstone fireplace and a small bedroom. Ten years later he bought the land and, according to the census taken in 1841, he had one hundred and twenty acres uncultivated and eighty acres cultivated.

The house and property remained in the family until 1951 when a niece, Mrs. Morse Ives, of Fairhope, Alabama, sold the farm to the Department of National Defence. At that time negotiations were initiated by Mrs. Hazel C. Mathews for acquisition of the house as an annex to the old Post Office Museum located at Lakeside Park. In 1955 the house was sold to the Oakville Historical Society for the sum of one dollar and relocated to the park beside the Post Office Museum.

The Thomas House is an intriguing small frame building exhibiting a settler's house in the simplest fashion. The exterior is finished in flushboarding under the porch, probably the end boarding with the fine beaded edge being the original. Windows are small, the glass seven by nine inches in sash of six panes over six. The roof has been restored in wood shingle, the fireplace and chimney reconstructed in the local river stone. The simple chamfered columns to the porch look a little heavy for the one-and-a-half-story house, and the low clearance gives a diminutive appearance to the whole.

54

Richard Brown

The Martin Homestead

MILTON

Sailing from Newcastle, England, on May 17, 1818, Jasper and Sarah (Coates) Martin arrived at York in August with their sons, four-month-old Joseph and John, not quite three. Sarah and Jasper were twenty-one years of age. They resided in York for three years while Jasper drew from the Crown one hundred acres of land in Milton. In October of 1822 the family settled on this property and purchased an additional one hundred acres from Joseph Whitefield.

Jasper built a grist mill by erecting a frame building beside the waters of the Sixteen Mile Creek. A few years later the building was replaced by a stone one with a sawmill, ashery, and store added. By damming the creek an artificial millpond was created. The mill soon became a focal point, attracting settlers who stayed and formed a small community known as Martin's Mill. The name later was changed to Milltown until 1838, when a public meeting was held and the name Milton accepted.

Jasper and Sarah had three other children, two sons, Edward and William, and one daughter, Hannah, who died in infancy. William drowned in the millpond in 1846 at age twenty-one.

John Martin married Margaret Hums in 1837 and twenty years later built a stone house for his wife and family. *The Halton Journal* of June 5, 1857, reported: "The spacious stone house in progress by John Martin will excel all residences of Milton in point of size, position and convenience.

It stands on an elevation which commands an excellent view of the town and a wide range of the country round, presenting one of the most fascinating panoramic sketches attainable in this neighbourhood."

In 1871 the Martin millpond became the scene of an amusing incident concerning ducks. Over the years the pond had become a sanctuary for birds that were protected by local game laws. One day three prominent young men, William Panton, Eugene Smith, and Archie McIntyre, were summoned to court to answer charges laid by Joseph Martin for shooting a duck in the pond. They admitted to the shooting of the duck but proof was lacking that the bird was wild. Joseph Martin and Charles Racey declared under oath that it was. While the case was being heard, William Panton carefully unwrapped a parcel containing the mangled remains of a tame duck. Mr. Martin, much to his own disgust, was unable to prove that this was the duck that was shot on the pond. The case was dismissed and Panton walked out of the court with the duck under his arm. Joseph Martin returned home and stated that henceforth all pleasure-seekers would be barred from walking along the millpond until time and circumstance should produce a change.

John Martin drowned in the creek in 1871 at the age of fifty-six. His house was sold in 1880 and remained in private hands until the town of Milton purchased it in 1977 for office space.

This handsome stone house is typical of the fine building of the area when Milton became the county seat of the newly formed Halton County. It is a strictly formal composition, mainly of the classical tradition, a five-bay front of two stories and a low-pitched hip roof with end chimneys. But a slight embroidery is already occurring in the projecting center bay with its gable decorated with a finial in the Gothic manner, and possibly at one time with a small-scaled but lace-like bargeboard. The entrance, a typical design of the mid-century with transom and sidelights, is further emphasized by the segmental arched window above, still with its original divided sash giving a clear indication of the fenestration to the rest of the front. Both the main front, facing south to a beautiful prospect over the millpond, and the east "front" facing the street are finished in a roughly tooled squared stone, ornamented with string course above the foundation and ruticated quoins at the corners. Elsewhere the stonework is broken-coursed rubble. Chimneys are a characteristic local design with a flared stone cap.

The Murray Homestead

North of Milton in the old township of Esquesing is the Scotch Block, an area of land once covered in tall pines, with some sections producing excellent stone for houses and fertile land for farming. The township derived its name from the pine timber and the name the Indians call it, meaning "land of the tall pines." The Scotch Block signified the "land of the Scotch" because it was first settled between 1817-19 by Scottish immigrants who secured the land in the southwest part of Esquesing. The immigrants all received one-hundred acre tracts to settle.

By 1821 the population of the township had reached four hundred and twenty-four. Life was a struggle without oxen or sleighs and the men had to travel on foot the forty miles to York with their flour. The journey took two days along the forest trails. Tools and implements for farm work were few, and these had to be brought a great distance. Mrs. David Darling of the township once carried a tub of butter to York and traded it for a logging chain, which she carried back with her.

The Murray family was one of the original settlers, with Robert Murray of Moffat Dumphfries, Scotland, settling on Lot 5, Concession 4, about 1817. Irregular stones were skillfully shaped by hand to produce the handsome fieldstone home. Murray included numerous windows to provide natural lighting and a view of the rolling countryside from all aspects. The interior featured a continuation of the exterior construction in the fieldstone fireplace, which provided the sole source of heat for the single room on the first floor and the two bedrooms above.

Murray and his wife had five sons, Robert, James, Nathanael, Wiliam, and Robbie. By 1860 the homestead was too small to accommodate a large family so they built a two-story brick house. However, instead of abandoning the old homestead, the Murrays attached the two houses and occupied both. They now lived in greater comfort in eleven rooms.

The *Atlas of the County of Halton* describes the township as a place where many of the farmers are wealthy and the township wears an air of thrift and prosperity. It is studded with handsome residences and had some very fine churches, among which the most notable are the Presbyterian and the Anti-Burgher churches in the Scotch Block.

The Murrays' son, James, the only one in fact to attain adulthood, was married three times. His first wife, Isabella Gillies, died in 1894 and second wife, Jennie, died in 1902. His third wife, Margaret Campbell, was ninety-five when she died in 1954. One daughter and one son were born from the three marriages. It was Stuart Murray, born 1893, who continued to live in the homestead and to operate the farm. He married Mary Fleming in 1923 and continued residence until he sold the farm in 1944.

The Murray Homestead is now owned by Mary and Bob Merry, who continue to work the land.

The Murray Homestead is a small stone, story-and-half house. This is the original five-bay house facing south and now overlooking a tranquil scene and the farm pond. A large stone base at the west end suggests the location of a former kitchen hearth. The "front" door is a six-panel design, the doorcase with a small-paned transom above indicating that other sash must have once been divided into smaller glass originally. Several six-panel doors survive, of the type with molded carcass and panels deeply fielded on one side, still with old thumb latches of the Norfolk pattern but with a transitional handle, possibly of the 1830s, with the back flattened. Old dormers occur on the house, with "stomacher" windows set near the floor having old sash of six panes set over three, the smaller unit alone and movable.

The Barber Homestead

In 1820 Georgetown bore the name of Hungry Hollow. The settlement consisted of three families growing their own food, making their own clothes, and barely scraping a living from the wilderness. The pioneers needed help and the Barber family was on the way.

The Barbers left Belfast in May of 1822 and arrived sixty days later in Quebec. The family, consisting of father, mother, four sons, and one daughter, then traveled by boat to the settlement of Prescott. There, Joseph Barber found employment in his trade as a bricklayer and stonemason. Since there was no building during the winter, he moved with his family to Niagara on December 12, 1822. About this time William Lyon Mackenzie was criticizing the government for allowing United States paper to be imported. In 1825 he called a meeting, and a proposal was put forth that the legislature award a five-hundred dollar bounty to the first man to establish a paper mill in Upper Canada. A petition was drawn up and the legislature passed an act on January 30, 1826, offering payment to the man who produced the first sheet of paper.

James Crook, who was building an industrial center at Crooks Hollow, three miles west of Dundas, decided to build the first paper mill. He traveled to Niagara and there engaged Joseph Barber as a stonemason and offered employment to his four sons. Crook won the bounty offered for the first sheet of paper. His rivals argued that he won only because he started the mill on a Sunday.

When Joseph Barber died in 1831, at Crook's Hollow, the Barber brothers decided to move on and set up business for themselves. They traveled by lake boat to Port Credit and walked up the Credit River to Hungry Hollow. There they purchased land and started up a woollen business and iron foundry. In time each brother built a house for himself. William Barber built this charming house shortly after arriving in Georgetown. Originally the building appeared smaller with a grand front verandah and conical roof. Sitting out on the verandah, William could gaze across the countryside and watch the Credit River flow. When William sold the house, new owners renovated and built additions, destroying its original appearance.

After carrying on their business for thirty-nine years without any deed of partnership or division of profits, the brothers agreed to make a settlement and separate in 1869. William and Robert bought the woollen business at Streetsville while Joseph and Bennett Franklin retired and James purchased the paper mills, which his son John continued to operate.

William Barber's homestead became the property of Alexander MaClaren in 1921. After his death the homestead passed on to his son Douglas MaClaren and his wife Irene, who are still residing there.

Crowning a hilltop, the Barber House has a magnificent prospect to the north and over the valley with its mill to the east. It is two stories high and made of large red brick similar to English brick and laid in common bond. Sills and lintels are of vertically tooled sandstone. The front has five bays, the center projecting very slightly to frame the doorcase with sidelights and transom originally filled with a rectangular chinoiserie of muntins. This center feature has a steeply pitched gable, at one time with a bargeboard and sporting a protective part octagon pagoda or bowed roof on brackets to shelter a small balcony from the second floor, perhaps originally with French windows from the upper hall. The house still has its original twelve-paned windows, many with the original much-distorted glass. The most interesting details are the cornices, the main gables with eaves returns, all ornamented with dentils terminated in half-acorn pendants. The form of the returns suggests a built-in cornice gutter, now removed.

Casa Loma

TORONTO

The dream of owning a castle begins for many as child's play on the ocean's shores, building dwellings from grains of sand. Sir Henry Mill Pellatt, born in Kingston, Ontario, in 1859, knew his castle in the light of reality, only to lose it in the changing tide of fortune.

A shrewd businessman, Sir Henry was only seventeen when he joined his father in the stockbroking business. He made his fortune by investing in the Northwest Land Company because he foresaw a time when the west would open up. By 1905 he had made frequent visits to Britain and continental Europe, always collecting sketches and details of magnificent castles that appealed to him. As in the days of King Arthur, Sir Henry, a knight, required a castle, and a castle he did build.

Construction of Casa Loma began in 1911, and was completed in 1914. Stonemasons from Scotland were employed to build the ninety-room castle with intricately carved fireplaces, stately towers, exquisite windows, and detailed doorways styled after many dwellings in Europe.

The interior was a salute to overindulgence with its European hand-loomed tapestries, hand-wrought silver, original oils, uniquely woven rugs, and stylish furnishings. The library was built to accommodate 100,000 volumes. The elaborate drawing room, paneled in fine French oak, took three European artisans three years to fashion. Lady Pellatt's suite, measuring three thousand square feet, included sitting rooms, bedroom, sun-room, and bathroom of soft-toned Italian marble with gold-plated fixtures. A balcony located off the suite provided a panoramic view of the city below. A castle without a great hall would be unheard of, and Sir Henry's had sixty-foot ceilings supported by laminated oaken beams and featured a four forty-foot windowcase with a total of 783 lights of glass.

The castle, set on twenty-five acres surrounded by four hundred varieties of trees, shrubs, and plants, had its own private telephone system, a fountain in the palm room, and a marble swimming pool. An underground tunnel ran from the basement under the road to the palatial stables.

Sir Henry then decided to venture into real estate to recoup his money. With the advent of war, people were forced to invest their sums in war bonds and industry. Sir Henry slowly lost his fortune and his empire collapsed. Weary of the expense of maintaining Casa Loma, Sir Henry turned his castle over to the city in 1924. A public auction was held and the treasures of Sir Henry Pellat were sold to the highest bidder.

In 1937 the Kiwanis Club of West Toronto, Inc., struck an agreement with the city to restore and operate Casa Loma as a tourist attraction. During the 1950s the Kiwanis Club hosted great social parties offering the finest entertainment around. Casa Loma for a time became a popular dancing spot for Toronto residents. The great doors of Casa Loma still remain open to curious tourists wishing to catch a glimpse of one man's dream.

Casa Loma is a superb example of an architect whimsically humoring the whims of a client who had an insatiable appetite for grandeur and an eclectic taste for the evocatively antique. How often must E. J. Lennox, an eminent Toronto architect, have been at his wit's end when presented with yet another idea by Sir Henry Pellatt. This extraordinary pile of stone was a very expensive enterprise—Sir Henry went broke and it was never finished. But it has survived to become a showplace of the city, one of the few Canadian chateaus which is not a hotel. The interior is in some areas sumptuous, in others cold and vast: it is hardly a house anyone today would call "home." Fascinating though it is, it lacks the whimsical audacity and exquisite charm of Prinny's Pavilion at Brighton.

Drumsnab

TORONTO

Drumsnab (meaning "round hill") is said to be one of the oldest residences still standing in Toronto. The building of Drumsnab by George Playter took place prior to 1812.

When Playter arrived in Canada from Maryland he received a grant of land adjoining the town of York. The land was a long hundred-acre stretch on the east side of what was later named Yonge Street, from Lot Street (now Queen), to Bloor Street. He also purchased a further hundred acres on the north side of Bloor Street from Yonge to Broadview. Each tract of land, as shown on the 1799 survey map was one and one quarter miles long by six hundred and sixty feet wide.

Originally Drumsnab was an eight-room colonial cottage with pine floorboards, a fieldstone cellar, and an encircling verandah. Playter selected a most picturesque location overlooking the Don Valley. Surrounded by fields and woods, Drumsnab perches near the edge of a slope, where the waters of Lake Ontario can be seen from a distance. Below the slope a stream flowed from the west side. Rising in the midst of the valley was a singular cone-shaped mound of earth covered with moderate-sized trees. The settlers named this magnificent creation of nature Sugar Loaf.

A good friend of Governor Simcoe, Playter induced him to build his home, Castle Frank, to the south. Lady Simcoe often visited the Playters at Drumsnab.

In 1834 the Playter family sold the house to Francis Cayley. A literary and artistic character, Cayley painted scenes of Faust in the principal room of the house. In the hallway he painted a floor-to-ceiling hatrack with his hat, cloak, and walking stick. At the time he stated, "As long as Drumsnab stands my hat and cloak will hang in the front hall." A whimsical representation of the Cayley motto, drawn over the living room door, showed a cat peering around a great wheel of cheese with an orchestra of mice and a number of mice dancing on the cheese. The motto stated, "When the cat's away the mice will play."

Francis's younger brother John moved into Drumsnab in 1847 with his wife, Clara Louisa Boulton of the Grange. In 1850 a second story designed by an architect friend of the Boultons was added to Drumsnab. It is quite probable that the gatehouse that once stood at the southeast corner of Parliament and Bloor was constructed at this time.

Drumsnab was sold in 1874 to Maunsell Bowers Jackson and another wing added to the house in 1910, when his daughter Rosalie Ann and her husband, Rueben B. Morley, moved in. Their son John Morley sold Drumsnab to M. F. Feheley in 1965. Mr. Feheley purchased the house on the condition that he would restore it to its former elegance which he did. Drumsnab now stands with a new lease on life.

Drumsnab is another composite of considerable interest, hardly recognizable from the colonial cottage of George Playter with its high-hipped roof descending over an encircling verandah. It appears that the succeeding owner had much to do with its renovation and enlargement so that now it exhibits a great deal more of the taste of the mid-nineteenth century. Some of the older detail does survive, such as the odd mantelpiece and interior trim, but both its external form and general proportions are now early Victorian.

The McQuay Homestead

PICKERING

Coming from Tyron, Ireland, about 1843, James McQuay eventually landed in York. Looking for a place to homestead with his wife Sarah, he headed east on foot. At the village of Pickering he turned north, hoping to find rich fertile fields to grow his crops. After trekking a few miles he found what he was looking for. There before him were two hundred acres of land on Lot 6, Concession 3.

McQuay first erected a log cabin for shelter and started to clear the land. He was soon able to build a delightful-looking frame house. In order to enhance and shelter the house from the wind he planted a row of pine trees in front. To build such a home was costly to a man beginning a new life in a country foreign to him. James solved the problem by working during the evenings, cutting timber off adjoining property for twenty-five cents a night. In time he was able to assemble his sturdy house and provide spacious bedrooms, kitchen, living room,

and parlor for his growing family. About the time his home was completed and barns erected James donated the northwest corner of his land for the construction of a school.

During the 1880s the McQuay family hosted an annual Strawberry Festival. Everyone would stop what they were doing and gather at the McQuay homestead for a day of socializing and dancing to the sound of a fiddle. The festival was usually held during the strawberry-picking season and everyone took turns hosting the festival.

Eventually the McQuay family left the homestead in 1894. Since then many owners have come and gone, everyone having changed the house a little to suit his tastes. A few years ago the entire house was stuccoed over, covering the natural wood. A construction firm now owns the house and property. Although the house is still lived in, its fate is uncertain.

The house, set back on the south side of the road, is a story and a half high with a gable roof and end chimneys. The walls are now finished in roughcast, and there is a long porch across the north front. A wing to the rear, housing the kitchen, forms a T, partly filled in at the southeast angle by a single-story lean-to. The most interesting feature is the strange asymmetrical front with two entrances — that to the left with a single window to one side; the other toward the west and set slightly off center between two windows. The windows, in sash of six panes over six, and the four-panel entrance doors with heavy projecting bolection molds suggest a date in the 1840s or early 1850s. The porch, with its heavy posts rather reminiscent of turned wooden pumps and fretted brackets in bold arabesques, suggests a slightly later improvement.

Inverlynn

WHITBY

William Laing arrived in Whitby in 1841 and established himself in business with his brother James. He later branched out on his own and soon operated the largest mercantile and grain business in the county. In 1859, the year he bought the land to build Inverlynn, he ran for Parliament against Premier Oliver Mowat and lost. Seemingly undaunted by his political failure, Laing ran for mayor of Whitby in 1863 and won.

Inverlynn was well suited to a gentleman of wealth. Surrounded by fifty acres of ornamental grounds the house cost upward to five thousand dollars to build. It measured forty-four by thirty-eight feet with a wing extending northward fifty by twenty feet. The interior was handsome, with marble mantelpieces, high ceilings, and spacious rooms, including a double drawing room on the east side. The winter kitchen built in the rear wing had servants' quarters above. Extending beyond was the summer kitchen with a storage room over it. An interesting feature of Inverlynn is the staircase rising from the back of the hall toward the front of the house. The hall with its great depth and gentle light filtering down from the Venetian window over the front door tends to draw the eyes up toward the window when you are ascending the stairs.

According to local legend, when Laing built Inverlynn in 1860, a grove of pine trees was planted nearby. When the wind rose, a haunting whisper would echo through the trees, frightening his wife. Fearing this eerie sound, she urged her husband to sell their new residence.

Unable to persuade her husband to sell Inverlynn, Louisa Laing settled down to enjoy the environment. On September 19, 1864, she gave birth to twin boys and died shortly afterwards, as did one of the twins. Her funeral procession numbered over ninety-eight carriages, composed of clergy, gentry, and representatives of most Whitby families and the surrounding neighborhood. Shutters were put up on stores in Whitby and places of business closed during the procession through the streets. Sadly stricken and faced with a large family to raise, William sold Inverlynn the next year, leaving behind the cherished home he built for his wife and family.

Inverlynn was purchased in 1870 by George McGillivary, a prominent businessman, and has remained in that family ever since. Mr. and Mrs. H. R. Schell now own Inverlynn, Mrs. Schell is a direct decendant of George McGillivary.

The only significant change is the replacement of the original verandah. In the early 1900s the bowed-roof verandah with trellis posts encircling the house and subduing the light through the many windows was removed and a straight-roof verandah with the heavy columns of the early twentieth century took its place along the front.

Inverlynn, a two-story hipped-roof house with end chimneys and generous windows, is part of a remarkably long-lived pattern in southern Ontario. It is a later version, still well proportioned, dignified, and serene in its setting on a plateau above Lynde Creek. The three-bay front has a center doorway with sidelights and square-headed transom, the door itself a single panel design with prominent bolection mold and inset panel mold of bead and reel repeated in the reveals of the recess. The brickwork is the familiar Flemish bond to front and, lane side to the east, the red ground ornamented with buff on "white" quoins, flat arches, and plinth above the stone foundation.

The Conant Homestead

OSHAWA

On October 15, 1792, Roger Conant landed on Canadian soil at Newark (now Niagara-on-the-Lake) after crossing the Niagara River on a flat-bottomed scow ferry. Journeying eastward along the north shore of Lake Ontario, he arrived in Darlington and there hastily built a log dwelling before winter set in. After blazing some eight hundred acres, Roger chose to become a fur trader with the Indians. After amassing a considerable fortune, he left his spacious and comfortable log cabin in 1811 and built a frame house near Oshawa harbor. Little did Roger know that his home would play a part in the War of 1812, a year later.

When General Hull surrendered his whole command of two thousand, five hundred men at Detroit, on August, 15, 1812, a serious question arose. What would the British do with so many prisoners? The redcoats decided to send the American prisoners to Quebec. Not being able to furnish them with boats, many were compelled to walk along the shore of Lake Ontario. The prisoners and guards were fed at various places along the route. When they arrived at Roger Conant's house without warning, the family quickly set a large pot of potatoes on the fire to boil. Fortunately a churning of butter had been done that day and a ham had been boiled the preceding day. The guards were outnumbered two to one, but no one escaped while feasting at this home.

A few days before Roger Conant died in 1821, he buried his gold in a large iron bake kettle on the bank of the salmon creek. When the kettle was missed from its accustomed position by the open fireplace, a search began but failed to reveal its whereabouts. Many have attempted to recover this buried treasure, but all have failed.

During the uprising of 1837-38, known as the Upper Canada Rebellion, Roger's son Daniel and his family resided in the house. One winter's night of 1837, at midnight, a Colonel Ferguson arrived at the Conant home and had his men surround the residence. The Conants were turned out into the snow while their house was ransacked and searched. Those were gloomy days for men whose lives and liberties were unsafe in Canada.

The Conant Homestead was also the birthplace of Thomas Conant, one of Canada's famous writers and author of *Upper Canada Sketches* and *Life in Canada*. The homestead remained in the Conant family until it was sold to the city of Oshawa in 1959. Prior to this, Mrs. Verna Conant wished to move the house down to the park by the lake among Oshawa's other historic buildings, but her wish was never granted by the city. The house could not be saved and the land was required for future development. In 1959 the Oshawa Fire Department arrived at the homestead and burned the building to the ground.

Today, few buildings of stylish architecture and historical significance remain standing in Oshawa. The land where the Conant house once stood still remains vacant, leaving all to wonder about future development.

This story-and-a-half frame house, with its long, single-story side wing obviously housing a kitchen and summer kitchen, is typical of the houses of the pre-War of 1812 period. The front appears to be a asymmetrical, the side with an odd arrangement of windows, the gable ornamented, probably with a false fan. End chimneys crown the gables, another marks the cooking hearth, and the one on the end of the wing may have served as a stove, used in the summer or for other essentials, such as bake oven or boiler.

Dundurn

BOWMANVILLE

The building of Dundurn began in 1853 when Reverend Alexander MacNab arrived in Bowmanville. On the outskirts of town he chose to build an impressive brick house in the Gothic Revival style, considered by many to be a country villa.

Complemented by spacious grounds, the house was called Dundurn, reputedly after Reverend MacNab's ancestral home in Scotland. His illustrious relative, Sir Allan MacNab, Prime Minister of the United Canadas from 1854 to 1856, had earlier built a home in Hamilton and named it Dundurn.

Reverend MacNab's Dundurn has an upper-story gable in the center of the front façade and a similar gable on the back side. The gingerbread, or bargeboard, on Dundurn is particularly light and lacy in character and unlike that used later in the century. Gothic motifs were used inside the house for the mantelpiece in the drawing room. Two pairs of French doors located on either side of the main entranceway led onto an open verandah overlooking the grounds.

Born in Upper Canada in 1811, Reverend MacNab became a deacon in the Anglican church of Coburg in 1850. A year later he advanced to the priesthood and served as the Anglican pastor around Rice Lake. Shortly thereafter, he moved to Newcastle to minister to Darlington and Clarke townships. During 1853 the two townships became separate charges and MacNab moved to Bowmanville to serve as the Anglican minister for the town and Darlington Township until his death in 1891.

The house became too large for Alexander MacNab and his wife after their six children had grown up, so in 1867 he sold Dundurn to John Milne, a Scotsman who conducted a general-store and liquor business in downtown Bowmanville. A staunch Conservative, Milne ran for Parliament in 1863 and 1867 but failed to gain a seat. However, the banners still flew from Dundurn with Sir John A. Macdonald hosting a social gathering with tables stretched across the grounds, laden with turkeys, hams, fruit, and pastries. Sir John was a frequent guest at Dundurn.

Marjorie and William Morrison purchased Dundurn in 1951 and continue to reside there. For them, Dundurn serves as a residence furnished tastefully to reflect the comfort of home.

Dundurn is a story-and-a-half house, with a five-bay front, the entrance set in a projecting center. The house is deep, the east end extended in an ell to provide a kitchen wing. The main roof is a low-pitched gable, the verge ornamented with a delicate sweeping bargeboard with finial and drop at the peak. The chimneys are placed inside the plan. Walls are of local red brick, the front in Flemish bond properly constructed with closers or quarter bricks at openings and corners; the rest of the walls in common bond. Exterior ornament also includes heavy hood molds or Tudor labels to windows, including the French window to the balcony above the front door. Heavy columns and pergolas to the front, beveled glass to French windows and sidelights and transom to the entrance as well as the front door and side porte-cochère are all early twentieth-century "improvements."

Terralta Cottage

PORT HOPE

The birth of Terralta Cottage began with John Burns about 1859, originally appearing as a small, handsome two-story brick dwelling covered with shingles laid in mortar. Situated on the north side of Dorset Street in Port Hope, it was set on a hillside surrounded by a white picket fence, and faced out over Lake Ontario.

Thomas Moore Benson, a Port Hope lawyer, purchased Terralta in 1868. Extensive renovations and additions began in 1874, when a south wing was added and the bargeboard on the west gable removed and reset in the south gable. The cupboards in the drawing room were lowered to the height of the doors. Doors and windows were removed and rooms enlarged.

Benson, an ardent admirer of the Right Honorable Sir John A. Macdonald, never entered politics although he was urged to do so by Sir John. In 1882 he was appointed deputy judge of the counties of Northumberland and Durham, and senior judge five years later. Eight years after the death of his first wife Mary in 1866, he married Laura A.

Fuller, second daughter of Bishop Fuller.

After the death of Thomas Benson in 1915, and his wife in 1923, the house passed on to their daughter Clara Cynthia Benson, professor of food chemistry at the University of Toronto.

Clara Benson had the interior of Terralta remodeled and added a ornamental tower to the front of the house, giving it a castle-like appearance. Clara's interest in Port Hope never flagged. She often assisted in the educational and cultural welfare of the community and served as honorary president of the local branch of the Ontario Architectural Conservancy.

Terralta Cottage, is now owned by Patrick Daniel, a great-grandson of Thomas Moore Benson. As is the case with many old homes, Terralta has been divided into rented apartments. The interior, losing all fashionable perspective, is in need of restoration. The exterior, which looks majestic, is slowly fading as time passes and shrubbery grows taller.

This house started out as a modest cottage ornee, distinctly of the Gothic Revival, its picturesque silhouette emphasized by the curious dormers with a hipped gable like a coif. The house was then enlarged and adorned with a later version of the ornamental tower to create a curious hybrid, still loyal to Gothic ornament but confused with the trappings of the Italianate, and evolving into a not unpleasant and rather amusing historic eclecticism best explained by the term Victorian.

Penryn

PORT HOPE

While the pioneer on land cleared a path through virgin timberland to allow for new settlement, another breed of pioneer fought to secure the waterways to ensure the safe passage of others. Such a man was Commander John Tucker Williams. Born in 1789, he left Cornwall, England, at an early age to join the Royal Navy and served as midshipman under Nelson at Copenhagen in 1801. A draft of naval officers came in Kingston in May, 1813, for service and Lieutenant Williams was among them. He served in the Lower Lakes until 1816, when he was transferred from HMS *Netley* to the Upper Lakes. In October he was appointed commander of the schooner, *Surprise.*

The following year Commander Williams retired from the Navy and left for England, but returned to Upper Canada in a year, bearing with him a dispatch from the Earl of Bathurst to the Duke of Richmond authorizing a grant of land to be given to him in proportion to his rank. He received by patent from the Crown a number of properties in the county of Durham and in 1829 established a homestead comprising one hundred acres in Port Hope. He named the house Penryn, after the village in which his parents had been married in England in the late 1700s. The house was built of lumber cut on the property and sawn at the mill on the Ganaraska, then known as Smith's Creek. The bricks for the fireplaces and chimneys were made in Port Hope. At a later date the entire house was bricked over and a square tower replaced the portico and balcony, and a fan-

light was removed. A wing on the west end was built, bay windows added and the window sashes changed. Two octagon-shaped summerhouses were built on the grounds and remain standing today, although in different locations.

Especially interesting is the oval room built off the upstairs landing at the head of the fine staircase. Commander Williams built the room as a replica of a ship's aftercabin, with gently sloping deck. The original stairway was a central gangway, rising from the center of the main hallway. There was an exceedingly fine ship's baluster, which was subsequently removed.

The summer kitchen in the basement, complete with hearth and bake oven, had a cobblestone floor. To the left of this kitchen is a small room with a bookcase against the wall. When the bookcase is pulled gently, it swings out to reveal a hidden vault where important papers and jewels were once stored.

In 1841 Williams ran for the Parliament of Upper Canada to represent the united counties of Durham and Northumberland. His campaign met with success and one of his first acts as a member was to introduce a bill that became law, granting the first copyright in Canada for a published book. He held office until 1848, and in 1850 became the first mayor of Port Hope. He died four years later at the age of sixty-five.

The Penryn estate is one of Port Hope's oldest homes and is still maintained as a private residence, owned by Jim and Lois Anderson.

The original design of this two-story house with hipped roof and chimneys is still easily recognized from the lakeside front, its principal façade of five openings with a center doorway. But considerable renovation to the north front, to the newer driveway access, and various improvements to add a wing and change the south front have somewhat compromised the simple formality of the house. At least one interior feature of note has been preserved, namely an oval drawing room on the second floor.

Strathmore

COBOURG

Cobourg is believed to have been first settled in 1798 by Eliud Nickerson. Earlier settlers had avoided the area because of its low, flat terrain with cedar stumps and creeks winding in great arcs approaching Lake Ontario.

In time, settlers began to arrive in considerable numbers, with many respectable English, Irish, and Scottish families making the society of Cobourg equal to any in the province. By 1854 the citizens felt certain that their prosperous community, with its well-constructed harbor and rapidly increasing population, was destined to be a great city. Grand homes rose up to reflect this feeling of success and future growth. In the late 1870s George M. Clark of Cobourg built a spacious mansion for his wife and family. Their home, called Strathmore, certainly suited the period of elegance and grace created by the American summer homes of this period.

George Clark, who served as junior judge for the county court of Northumberland and Durham,

later became involved in a number of government commissions of enquiry, including the investigation into all transactions of the Canadian Pacific Railway. By 1886 he was solicitor general of the Canadian Pacific Railway.

Strathmore remained unchanged until 1905 when Charles Donnelly, an American industrialist, purchased it as a summer home. Wishing to enlarge its appearance to suit the Colonial Revival style, he built wings and porches on each end. Donnelly never lived to enjoy the fruits of his labor, for he died a year later, leaving his family to inherit his fortune and magnificent home. Strathmore remained in the Donnelly family until 1914, when the family declared bankruptcy and fled the house without their belongings.

In 1947 the Ontario government purchased Strathmore and turned the building into a training school for juveniles. Like so many buildings, Strathmore's splendor disappeared with time and the building stands as an aged monument to the past.

Strathmore exemplifies the evolution of a mansion during Cobourg's heyday as a summer resort. Started as a simpler house about 1870, it then grew, with porches and wings added and various improvements made to give it a distinctly turn-of-the-century, Colonial Revival flavor.

Ravensworth

COBOURG

At one time it was stated that every admiral in the American Navy had vacationed at least once in Cobourg. As the years passed, quite a number of wealthy American steel magnates from Pittsburgh arrived in this resort area. Soon old Cobourg residences were bought and enlarged and many new palatial homes erected in the style of Newport.

General Charles Fitzhugh was one of the wealthy Americans who built a summer home in Cobourg. He was born in Oswego, New York, in 1838 and later entered West Point Academy. When the young manhood of the nation was called upon to respond to a call to war. Charles Fitzhugh at once gave his services to his country and, after being in action a short while, received a commission as first lieutenant. Promotion followed quickly in the field and he soon became the youngest general in the Northern army.

He married Emma Shoenberger in 1865 and resigned from the army two years later. In 1900 he built Ravensworth, a stunning summer home on the shore of Lake Ontario. In keeping with the Colonial appearance, the grounds were laid out in a graceful manner, with elegant gardens immaculately groomed. Ravensworth was to become the scene of great family gatherings and the marvelous social events of a summer society. Lavish dinner parties reflected the architectural formality of the house, softened by the sweeping curves of gowns and softly curled hair, by light laughter, by a cigarette tucked into a long gold holder held at a slightly upward tilt, the smoke gently curling toward the high ceilings as people flowed from one room to the other. Music and dancing continued until dawn, with crystal chandeliers glittering in the rays of the morning sun.

Both the general and his wife died in 1923 and their summer home was sold to Richard Baylor Hickman of Kentucky. Ravensworth was soon to become the scene of an attempted assassination. One evening Hickman was sitting in his library quietly reading a book when suddenly a bullet whistled through the air and lodged itself into the wall paneling three inches above his head. Hickman raced out of the house to search the grounds but was unable to find the culprit. He retired for the night with the intention of notifying the police in the morning. Sometime during the night the would-be assassin returned and entered the library and removed the bullet from the wall. He was never found.

Ravensworth is now owned by Mr. and Mrs. J. Peters and remains virtually unchanged, still appearing in all its splendor as a reminder of an earlier era of elegance.

Ravensworth was built as the summer residence of an American family—an expression of architectural taste essentially American, too, a version of the Neo-Classic of the early twentieth century. In this example the architect relies on rather liberal interpretations of Greek Revival and Colonial. Comparable examples can be seen along the sea coast of new England, especially in Maine.

The Maples

GRAFTON

In winter of 1944 Edward Webster, a young Canadian soldier, arrived in the village of Cold Kirby, England, searching for the birthplace of his forefather, Thomas Webster.

Thomas Webster, in 1822, at the age of thirty-six, left Yorkshire, England with his wife Barbara, his son William, and his daughter Elizabeth, and came to Canada, eventually settling in Grafton, Ontario. William grew up to marry Sarah Ann Hare in 1846; she died ten years later, leaving William with two daughters and one son. For the next eight years William's sister Barbara kept house for the family until he married Annie Clark on July 7, 1864. William was forty-three years old and Annie twenty-four.

Shortly before the marriage William built The Maples, a thirteen-room house with six bedrooms on the second floor and a mahogany bannister, perfect for sliding, which became the pride and joy of his children. A cookhouse was added in 1875. The house was constructed of bricks produced from a site located a half-mile north of the house and a half-mile south of Highway 2. William and Annie raised eight daughters and four sons, along with William's son and daughter from his first marriage. In time Thomas, son of William and Sarah Ann, married and continued farming at The Maples.

Farmers, so dependent on and vulnerable to nature's whimsical ways, often suffered great hardships. Thunderstorms could suddenly blot out the sun; hail could destroy ripening crops. The Websters were kept busy harvesting during the later summer months. Sometimes hired hands were hard to come by and acres of vegetables, oats, and wheat awaited attention. In his diary Thomas Webster wrote in 1875: "Friday, September 3rd. Drew in eighteen loads of oats from southeast field on Clark place.

"Tuesday, September 7th. Finished drawing in wheat then drew in nine loads of peas for father out of brickyard field. Went to the village in the evening to attend Father Chiniquey's lecture, but couldn't get in on account of the crowd. The town hall is so full that many could not get in. There was a fight in the street."

November arrived and the Websters continued plowing the fields with their teams of horses. By early December snow covered the frozen ground. "Saturday, December 18th. Clear and sharp. Father took two hogs to Cobourg and received $7.37½ per cwt.

"Saturday, December 25th. Mild, rained early in the morning with lightning and thunder. Uncle John and family here for Christmas. Brought grandfather over in the morning and took him back in the afternoon."

Edward Webster, the young soldier, found his family's birthplace that winter in 1944 and inspired by that success, he has continued a thirty-four-year search for his heritage.

This brick house was carefully sited to take advantage of the prospect from the knoll overlooking the shore and lake beyond. Hence the south front has French windows to the verandah, the main entrance being placed on the road side to the east. The front gable with its lacy bargeboard is a mid-nineteenth-century Gothic Revival touch, but the gable ends lack returns, the eaves have a sloped soffit common to the later period. The half-panes to the French windows are characteristic of the 1850s and '60s. Those to the east, beside the "front" door suggest that the verandah once wrapped around this side of the house too: the simpler Tuscan columns would indicate a turn-of-the-century or twentieth-century improvement.

The Whitehouse

BRIGHTON

In the year 1851 Brighton had a population of seven hundred, among them a new lawyer by the name of John Eyre. He was an ambitious man, assisting in founding the Union Agricultural Joint Stock Company at Clark's Hotel in 1873 and serving one term as a member of Parliament. About 1880 Eyre built a magnificent three-story Georgian house, complete with a full basement, triple brick walls, open porches to the east and west sides, and turreted tower. When Eyre died in 1889, nine years after having built his home, apparently no one in the family wished to keep the house and it passed into the hands of a trust company until 1898, when a grocer in Brighton, Samuel Nesbitt, bought it.

Nesbitt was both industrious and highly imaginative. He founded the Brighton Bicycle Club on May 15, 1896, in the back of his drygoods store. On April 24, 1896, he wrote a column called "Bicycle" for the *Brighton Ensign* newspaper. Partly a sales announcement, it stated: "Ladies and Gentlemen, I carry the largest stock of wheels in the country. I have selected these wheels that have given the best satisfaction in Canada and the United States." He later mentioned the names of people to whom he had sold wheels. On the list was Eleanor Bibby, a young lady who was soon to become his wife.

Nellie, as she was called, was described as being a very proper Victorian lady, somewhat severe in appearance but motherly by nature. Samuel and Nellie raised two daughters, Frances and Edith, and two sons, Edwin and Ernice. In the 1920s Samuel renovated the Whitehouse by stuccoing the outside

of the building and constructing a tower with windows overlooking his fifty-three acres.

Samuel's greatest contribution to Brighton and the country was a canning factory, which he established in 1894 under the auspices of Dominion Canneries. Being a progressive man, he also established a laboratory for the development of better qualities of fruits and finer methods of canning, including experimental work into the preservation of foods. According to the *Brighton Ensign* in 1902, 1,110,621 barrels of apples were exported to Europe and 202 to Japan.

Nellie died in 1929 and Samuel, aged sixty-nine, married her younger sister, Maria, a French teacher at Teacher's College in Toronto.

Samuel died in 1938 and the Whitehouse, known then as Grandfather's House, became Rene's Whitehouse Hotel. Rene was Irene Dickson's nickname. She managed the Nesbitt estate for the next thirty-four years, serving many celebrities at the hotel, among them Prime Minister William Lyon Mackenzie King, Mr. and Mrs. Walt Disney, and Irene Castle, a famous ballroom dancer.

The Whitehouse thrived as a business venture until Highway 401 was completed in the 1950s; after that, fewer travelers used Number 2 Highway. When Irene's health began to fail she sold the Whitehouse to Shirley and Bill Langer in 1973. Norman and Karen Clift purchased the Whitehouse from the Langers in 1979 and now operate it as a licensed dining lounge.

This pretentious villa is an obvious expression of wealth and position. Built on the western edge of town on a commanding site, it cannot help but attract the eye. The building is a strange medley of styles, partly explained by its turn-of-the-century "modernization," which added the much-divided eyebrow windows to the central tower and the generous porte-cochère. The brackets to the eaves and the very formal main block with its symmetrically disposed front and bay windows might easily be of the 1870s or even earlier, but the exaggerated steep-roofed tower places the building among the later versions of the popular Tuscan villa style. Here, it is definitely Victorian rather than Italianate.

Springbank

TRENTON

In 1853, after three years of transporting limestone on barges from Kingston to Trenton, James Cummings finished building his house. The seven-room dwelling, with two back kitchens, a center hallway, and a winding staircase of walnut, expresses a unique style of Ontario cottage architecture. James called his new home Springbank, since it was built on the crest of a hill overlooking the Bay of Quinte with a spring at the foot of the bank.

James had immigrated to Trenton from Perthshire, Scotland, in the early 1800s. Upon arrival he became involved in the lumbering business since Trenton, situated at the confluence of the River Trent and the Bay of Quinte, was an active lumbering center. He later managed the Gilmour Mills for some time and served as postmaster for many years.

About 1850 he married Margaret Amelia Wragg and began construction on Springbank. He served as reeve of Trenton in 1860 and again in 1867 to 1870. When the Bank of Montral opened its first branch in Trenton, James was appointed manager. He died in 1873 leaving his wife Margaret, daughter Flora, and two sons, Ross and Robert, to manage Springbank. Margaret married Daniel Murphy, and when she died in 1914 Springbank was passed on to Ross Cummings, who had married Agnes Devlin.

Living the life of a gentleman, Ross would pass the days by serving as a volunteer fireman and sailing his boat, *Surprise,* on the Trent River, often guiding tourists through the canal. Years earlier, his father had taken him to Quebec by boat and escorted him to McGill University in Montreal, where he wanted him to study. When James arrived back at the Trenton docks, he was met by Ross, who had decided not to stay and had traveled back home by land.

Agnes Cummings died in 1933, and when Ross died in 1940, he left Springbank to his two daughters, Laura and Angela. Angela had married Alfred Cullin, a stockbroker from London, England, in 1936, and after her father's death, they moved into Springbank with Laura. When Cullin died in 1949, Angela remained at Springbank with her sister.

In the winter of 1978 most of Springbank was torn down and the property sold to a land developer. The two sisters, not wanting to see all of Springbank demolished, decided not to sell all of the property. This allowed them to save a portion of the house. Angela, now eighty-seven, and Laura, ninety-four, still reside in the portion of Springbank saved from demolition.

All that remains of this fascinating "cottage" is the billiards room enlarged by an early twentieth-century second story in concrete block and the amputated stump of its connection with the house itself. The original house had a hip roof, sloping on all four sides, presumably with end chimneys. The projecting front dormer, forming a small tower, is unusual. But the low spreading form, the symmetrical front, and the elaboration of the entrance are all part of the vocabulary of the "Ontario cottage" in its more sophisticated expression.

The O'Rourke House

In 1884 Hugh and Mary O'Rourke, wanting to begin a new life, left County Carlow, Ireland, for Canada. Arriving in Trenton, Ontario, Hugh O'Rourke began a grain business and later served on town council.

His son Thomas Alfred, born in 1853, studied at St. Michael's College and Trinity College in Toronto. After graduating as a lawyer in 1878, he wanted to move to Cleveland, Ohio, but his parents persuaded him to return to Trenton. For the next ten years he served as a lawyer until he was appointed police magistrate, a position he held for the next thirty years.

Shortly after marrying Jessie Keith in 1882, Thomas began construction of a simple cottage for his parents on Queen Street. What began as a modest dwelling rose up to become a towering castle dominating the entire street with its formal appearance. The interior provided elaborate trim and flat decorative ceiling rosettes and heavy cornices. The main staircase with large newels and turned balusters rose up in a sweeping gesture of elegance. The slate roof of the house cast shadows on nearby trees in the afternoon sun. Thomas was so impressed by his own creation that he later resided there with his own family of nine children.

In the course of his business he assisted many private banks attempting to establish firm foundations in Trenton. By the early 1900s he had lost a sizable sum with his investments and sold his beautiful home.

Although the O'Rourke home remained a family residence for a number of years, it was eventually broken up into apartments, which exist today.

The story of the O'Rourke family is a fine example of an immigrant family leaving a traditional way of life and starting over again, followed by the next generation who received the finest education available and attempted to establish a new identity in a new land. The loss of a home was often experienced by honest men attempting to strengthen and develop the economy of the country.

Late Italianate would best describe this elaborate towered house with an ell-shaped plan. The projecting gable with pierced but heavy bargeboard, the tower roof of broached shape, cresting to rooftops and patterned brickwork are mid-Victorian just beginning to merge with the late period. The brackets to the tower cornice are of the 1880s, and the porch of even later vintage.

LINDSEY HALLAM 1978

The Johnston Homestead

HAVELOCK

John Johnston and his family, filled with the spirit of adventure, left Ireland to make a home for themselves in Canada. They journeyed to the township of Belmont in the county of Northumberland (now the county of Peterborough), near Havelock in 1830. With their seven sons and two daughters the Johnstons built a log house behind a spring, cleared the land, and cultivated as best they could among the stumps during the first year. The original Crown deed for one hundred acres was acquired November 25, 1840, at a price of forty-three pounds, fifteen shillings.

The Johnstons were among the first settlers in the township, which had not been surveyed until 1823. Nineteen years later, only thirty-three families lived there. One son, Thomas, went to Cavan to marry his bride, Mary Brennan, whom he had never met. Together they walked back on a blazed trail, Thomas carrying a bag of flour while Mary carried her cooking utensils and bridal apparel. Later, Mary became the midwife who delivered most of the babies in the area. Prior to the time of birth, someone in the family would come to see her. She would send them back with an herbal preparation to induce labor. The expectant mother would take this concoction and as the time of birth drew near, Mary would set out to be there in time for the delivery.

As time passed, the Johnston family acquired twenty-five hundred acres between Old Havelock and the Trent River. Old Havelock (later changed to Havelock) was the center of commerce in the last century. Mary and Thomas lived in the original log house until about 1873, when their unmarried sons, Sam and Joe, built a new brick one. The house took some time to build because they made their own mortar and lime, cut their logs for the saw mill, besides cutting three loads of body maple to exchange for one load of brick from the Campbellford brick yards. But when the house was completed, Thomas refused to move in, preferring the comfort of his log cabin.

A lady by the name of Mrs. Smith came to keep house for Joe and Sam. Her husband had been killed when a team of horses had run away while plowing. Eventually the brothers came to fight over Mrs. Smith's hand until she chose Joe. Following this, the brothers refused to speak to one another for forty years. They split the farm, then three hundred acres, between them. Neighbors would pass messages between the brothers.

Joe Johnston's only daughter, Elida, married George Rigby and remained on the farm until their son George took it over in 1942. He still resides on the farm with his family, sheltered from season to season in a house built by his forefathers.

The Johnston house stands on the high land to the west of the road, the long barn set behind it. Of red brick, it is a story and a half high with steeply pitched roofs and stove chimneys. The house is an ell plan, the angle filled in with a porch, which continues around the south side. A summer kitchen wing, now altered for modern convenience, was housed in a rear wing. The recessed section of the front has a gable with fretted bargeboard and pointed window lighting the capacious stairhall. Other windows are with segmental heads, sash-in two panes over two in the late Victorian manner, the front entrance with a transom, the upper part of the door glazed in round-headed panels and finished with large bolection molds. Verandah posts are stocky, but not heavy, chamfered designs, the head with an arch of fretted ornament of stock pattern. One curiosity is the brick bond with a Flemish course (alternating headers and stretchers or short and long bricks) occurring as the bond in every seventh layer.

Janet M'Ghee

The Stewart Homestead

HAVELOCK

About 1830 Robert Stewart arrived in the rugged countryside of Havelock, where the soil grows more rocks than weeds. He chose to settle there, where rolling hills and meandering streams were a fond reminder of his native Scotland. Setting forth on the Old Norwood Road, he spotted an appealing clearing and decided to purchase one hundred acres there. It is quite probable that he bought the land in the winter, not noticing how low and swampy one section of it was. On the most fertile section of his land, he grew potatoes, grain, and oats, allowing his sheep to graze elsewhere.

Robert first built a log shanty to protect himself from the cold. He married Barbara Nathason and fathered one son and three daughters. According to a descendant of the family, he moved several times on his property, each time building another dwelling. Robert died in 1881, the same year that his son built a handsome log house on the high ground for his wife Agnes Buchanan.

The house consisted of a large room with a combination cook-heat stove tucked in one corner. The main room, color-washed a light blue, had a central stairway leading to two bedrooms on the second floor. A trapdoor led from the main floor to the hand-dug dirt cellar below. Wood was stored in a shed attached to the west side of the house. This also provided an alternate entrance to the cellar. A well was dug near the cabin. An unusual-looking outhouse was located out to the rear.

The Stewart family continued to reside in this log house until they sold it in 1958. Their home had provided warmth, shelter, and an environment to grow. Still standing straight and tall, the Stewart homestead remains vacant, awaiting a new owner to come and save it.

Remote and forlorn, squatting on the nearest high ground to the road and down a long tree-lined lane, this small log house bespeaks the hardship of working the poorer stony land. The house began as the more basic dwelling of farm settlement, with a low, wide center door and window on either side facing south, two windows to the north and one to the east, all with sash of eight panes over eight. Upstairs in a half-story under a roof of medium pitch, with gables filled in with horizontal clapboard and a single window of six panes over six, was a sleeping loft.

Later a lean-to was added across the south front to spoil forever the innate charm of this simple building. The logs are probably of cedar like the large round tree trunks used to support the ground floor. But the corners are notched square, without self-draining dovetails locking the structure together and insecure unless vertical dowels were used between logs.

Janet M'Ghee

The Doxsee House

HASTINGS

The village of Hastings has remained a popular summer resort since it was incorporated in 1875. The Trent River flowing through the middle of the village and its potential water power enticed such pioneers as Benjamin and Roderick Doxsee to settle there. The two brothers had arrived in Hastings during the 1880s from Prince Edward County. Looking to venture into business, they chose the lumber industry and built a planing mill on Water Street.

By 1900 both men had achieved success through their milling operation and shrewd investments in stock. Now it was time for them to build themselves elegant houses to suit their taste. Both men obviously shared the same taste in architecture, for they built identical houses side by side on a hillside that overlooked the village. The twin houses, designed by New York City architect Stanley A. Dennis, certainly stood out from the other early classical homes on the street, looking like villas to house royalty instead of two lumber businessmen.

Unfortunately, only Benjamin's house remains untouched today. It features a parlor and sitting room to the right and dining room to the left, adorned with oak archways and paneling. The back kitchen at the rear has a stairway leading to the second floor and is shaded from sunlight by a porch looking out toward the carriage house, which the brothers shared. A handsome oak staircase leading off the main hallway leads to the five rooms on the second floor. The third floor consists of one large room used mainly for storage space.

A man of medium height characterized by a mustache and the tobacco he loved to chew, Benjamin served for many years as superintendent of the United Church Sunday School. In 1923 the Doxsee planing mill burned to the ground after being struck by lightning during an electrical storm. Soon afterward, Benjamin died, leaving his wife Sarah Thompson and his daughter and son to look after his estate. Eventually Sarah sold the house and moved her family to Detroit.

Few people in Hastings today remember the Doxsee brothers, and the tourists who stop in front of Benjamin Doxsee's house to take a picture never know that the house beside it was identical.

The Doxsee House is a typical example of the late Victorian villa, a summer house in black and white in the shingle style and dripping with all the eclectic stock ornament beloved of builders of the time. The house is an irregular outline with projections crowned by gables and a corner octagon tower with three stories, the rest of the house of two stories and an attic. The stories are divided by projecting skirts of shingles with dentil cornices, the tower having a bracketed upper cornice and conical roof of octagonal form, the front gable with a paneled band and ornamental shingling above, framing a much-divided attic sash, its center a diamond lozenge. Turned porch columns are of three distinct types, all elaborately late Victorian, from wasp-waisted shape to end-to-end vase form. But the tour de force of ornament occurs on the north side. Here a lozenge of circular pattern extended with lobes is filled in with a diaper of reeded trim, the center tile with an incised pattern—this picked out in black and white, like the double roundels having flailing sunbursts below.

Janet McGhee

The Willows

GORE'S LANDING

Few Canadians know the famous artist who built his summer home on the shore of Rice Lake. On January 20, 1845, one of Canada's most prolific but least-known painters, Gerald Sinclair Hayward, was born. A man of many talents, Hayward dared to pursue life to the fullest. For a while he was chief engineer aboard a prairie schooner on the Dakota Plains in the 1860s. Returning to Canada, he enlisted for frontier service with the Port Hope Infantry Company in November, 1865. He was awarded a Queen's Medal and discharged in April, 1866, with the rank of ensign. Next, he tried farming and railroading, but neither seemed to satisfy him. He was in his early twenties when he decided to approach an entirely new career.

The art of painting miniature portraits and scenes appealed to Howard, but it was not widely practiced in Canada, so he went to study at the Royal Academy schools in London in 1870. While there, he was commissioned by many members of the English, German, and Russian courts to do miniature portraits on ivory. He painted Queen Victoria, the Prince of Wales (later King Edward VII), Princess Alice, the Countess of Minto, the Duke and Duchess of Buckingham, Lord and Lady Caven, the Empress of Prussia, and the Czarevitch of Russia. Later, in Canada, he painted Prime Ministers MacDonald and Laurier.

Hayward gave the first exhibition of ninety modern miniatures in the United States at the Avery Galleries, New York, in 1889, and continued to exhibit throughout the country. One leading newspaper said: "Mr. Hayward has become world-famous in his exclusive field and has painted more than a thousand distinguished persons in America on coming out from London." Another wrote: "His work is strongly individualistic—the eye full of life, hair freely treated, fidelity in tint of complexion, with perfect harmony in tone of background, combine to make the living portrait possible to obtain."

Hayward took up residence in New York City, but returned to Canada to build a summer home in Gore's Landing on Rice Lake in 1900. The Willows was his favorite retreat, and he was so enchanted with the panoramic view from his tower window that he later painted the lake and its many islands on the walls of his dining room.

As church warden, Hayward assisted in the building of St. George's Anglican Church in the village, and much of its artistic appearance is due to his interest in the construction. When he died in New York on March 31, 1926, his ashes were brought to Gore's Landing by his daughter and buried in the cemetery of the church. The *Toronto Star Weekly* published an article on Hayward on April 3, stating, "In the passing of Gerald Sinclair Hayward, world-famous miniature painter, Canada loses one of her greatest artists." Unfortunately, he has been all but forgotten as a Canadian artist. The murals of Rice Lake on his dining room walls are now covered with two coats of paint, and his beautiful home, The Willows, is now known as Victoria Inn.

Towers as outlooks over lakes and country views are the marks of villas, summer houses, and resort hotels of the turn of the century. The Willows, a three-story wooden house designed by a New York architect, fits the pattern. The small oval window is another favorite device of Edwardian times. Generous windows provided sunlight and air to the bedrooms, and a wide stoop, often augmented by screened verandahs, gave space for relaxation and enjoyment of company.

The Hutchinson House

PETERBOROUGH

Not every community like Peterborough built its local doctor a house. In the year 1836 Dr. John Hutchinson, one of Peterborough's earliest medical men, had thoughts of moving elsewhere because he required better accommodations for his growing family. The town was still in its early stages of development, with fewer than one thousand settlers in small frame or log houses.

A native of Kirkcaldy, Scotland, Dr. Hutchinson had immigrated to Upper Canada in 1818. He first practiced medicine in the Rice Lake area and Port Hope before arriving in Peterborough in 1830.

He became a leading member of the community, and when word spread that the doctor was considering a move, the villagers held discussions and decided to offer to build him a house of stone, hoping this might persuade him to stay. Good quality brick was unavailable, and local legend has it that the people rallied round in the summer of 1836, bringing their teams to draw stone from a quarry northwest of the settlement. Local stonemasons, carpenters, joiners, glaziers, and roofers all gave their time plus materials to complete the job.

In February of 1837 Dr. Hutchinson and his family moved into the handsome stone dwelling. A parlor and a bedroom were to the right of the center hall; on the left was the study or consulting room, with another bedroom behind it. The kitchen was quite cosy with its color-washed stone walls and exposed beams. At first a ladder-like affair was used to reach the bedrooms on the second floor; later an open stairway was built.

In 1845 Sanford Fleming, a cousin of Dr. Hutchinson who would later become Chief Engineer of the Canadian Pacific Railway, inventor of Standard Time, and pioneer of the Canadian postal service, immigrated with his brother David and for the first two years resided with the Hutchinson family. Fleming's lifelong habit was to record each day's events in a journal. His first view of Peterborough prompted him to write: "rather poor, little place…stumps of trees still in the middle of the streets, a wood house here, with a few good villas with verandahs around, in the suburbs."

The Hutchinsons remained in the house nearly eleven years until the doctor contracted typhus from the immigrants he was tending during a disastrous epidemic in Upper Canada in 1847. His widow decided to join her relations in Toronto.

The house was bequeathed to the Peterborough Historical Society in 1969 by Jeanette Connal Brown, great-granddaughter of its second owner, James Harvey. On May 24, 1975, a major fundraising campaign was launched to support the cost of restoration. The Historical Society engaged restoration architect Peter Stokes to do the preliminary assessment of the building. Two years later the restored Hutchinson House was officially opened to the public by Her Honour Pauline McGibbon, Lieutenant-Governor of Ontario.

This story-and-a-half stone house occupies a sidehill position so that the kitchen in the east end of the basement is largely above grade, with a rear door at ground level. The house is a three-bay front, the doorway with sidelights, the casement sash restored to the windows. The roof is still a low-pitched gable. There are large end chimneys in stone serving the cooking hearth in the basement and the parlor above on the one side and the consulting room (as it is now called) opposite. In the early period there was also a small fireplace in the second floor. The front gable with its bold, looping bargeboard and those on the gable ends, coupled with the rather heavy porch, illustrates changes made about 1855 by the second family occupying the house, while the two-story brick wing to the rear is another addition of the 1870s.

The Purdy Homestead

LINDSAY

In 1827 three Americans, William Purdy and his sons, Jesse and Hazard, decided to build a dam, and they entered into a contract with the Canadian government to build a sawmill and a ten-foot dam on the Scugog River by 1828. A grist mill was to be completed the following year. For this they were to receive four hundred acres and a bonus of six hundred dollars.

The dam and the sawmill were completed in September of 1828. Everyone waited for the mill-pond to fill up—some thought within twenty-four hours—but the water failed to reach the top of the dam until the following April. The pressure on the dam that spring was too great, the center timbers shifted on the rock bottom of the river, and the dam was swept away. The Purdys received a time extension of one year and by April, 1830, the dam was rebuilt and the grist mill completed.

In 1834 John Huston of Cavan and a party of men arrived to plot out streets and lots near Purdy's Mill. One of Huston's assistants, Lindsay, was accidentally shot in the leg and the wound became infected. When he died, they buried him on the riverbank and this led to the townsite being called Lindsay.

The Purdy homestead, built about 1830, was destroyed by a fire that swept through the village in 1866. No record was kept to show the actual construction of the home, but since Purdy owned such a large tract of forested land it seems probable that he built his home of logs, cutting them in his own mill.

In the early 1830s William Purdy began opposing the Family Compact, a small group of wealthy Loyalists who comprised the governing class of the period. This led to his arrest and transport to the Cobourg jail. After several days he was released and told to mind his own buisness. Shortly afterward, in 1837, William and his son Jesse moved to Bath, Ontario. Hazard remained in Lindsay to operate the mill.

The Purdy dam had backed the waters of Scugog over some sixty thousand acres of land adjacent to the river and lake. The forests and all the vegetation began to rot and a plague of fever and ague occurred. Nearly one third of the population died and few men remained healthy enough to bury the dead. Hostility toward the dam grew with each death until a great band of farmers from nearby townships, armed with flintlocks, pitchforks, and axes, marched to Lindsay. Once there, they hacked away part of the dam. Hazard Purdy rebuilt it, but at a lower level.

Hazard Purdy sold the mill and the four-hundred-acre Purdy tract to Hiram Bigelow in the spring of 1844 and went to live in Pembina, North Dakota. A year later new mills were erected and the Purdy dam removed. The virtual founders of Lindsay had disappeared.

The Purdy house and several others in the same general area, of roughly the same date, share a common background, the Romantic Cottage. The influence is the Picturesque, a Regency flavor with Gothic seasoning to produce a house like a cottage with the upper half-story below a more steeply pitched roof than was common at the time. Entrances were not always in the center but perhaps even in the back wing where the stair hall was located. Fireplaces were sometimes clustered in the center of the house; French windows from the principal rooms opened to an encircling verandah supported on slender posts.

The Mackenzie Estate

KIRKFIELD

The setting, architectural style, and interior trim of a house often reflect the owner's character. This was true of Sir William Mackenzie, Canada's railroad baron, who built a stately brick house in Kirkfield, Ontario. The son of a Scottish immigrant born in 1849, Mackenzie began his railroad career with a contract to supply railway ties for tracks being laid in the area. In 1884 he received his first large contract involving the construction of a railway section in the Rocky Mountains for the Canadian Pacific Railway. While working on this project Mackenzie met Donald Mann, a subcontractor working on the next section of the CPR line through the Rockies. The two men, sharing a mutual bond of respect, decided to combine their individual talents.

Their first railroad was a one-track line running sixty miles from Dauphin to Winnipegosis in Manitoba. This railroad allowed grain to be shipped from the southern prairies to grain vessels for distribution to larger centers of population. They then decided to build a railroad across the northern prairies, using specialized equipment and methods that enabled them to lay a mile of track a day.

In 1877 Sir William built a forty-room mansion for his family. Lady Mackenzie was an avid gardener and often brought back exotic vegetation from Europe to enhance the landscape. She had a wooden water tower contructed near the house to provide an ample supply of water for her gardens. Sir William built a nine-hole golf course on the property.

Lady Mackenzie was extremely sensitive about the appearance of Kirkfield, and if a home did not appear respectable, it was not unusual for a crew of men to arrive one day to paint the house at her ladyship's expense.

In 1911 William Mackenzie and Donald Mann were knighted by King George V. By that time their assets and holdings amounted to billions. A year later they decided to expand their northern railway coast to coast. They invested their fortune in this enormous project, but millions more dollars were needed. The Canadian government was reluctant to lend money to railroad barons, but finally agreed, with stringent conditions attached. The terms became too difficult for any man to meet, and the government foreclosed when the company defaulted on a payment in 1916. A year later Mann and Mackenzie had lost everything. The government took over operations, changing the name from Canadian Northern to Canadian National. At the time of his death in 1923 Sir William Mackenzie had little wealth.

His family gave his estate to the Sisters of St. Joseph. The house became a boarding school and later a retreat until 1976, when the Sisters sold the property to Mr. and Mrs. D. MacDonald-Ross. The Mackenzie house was then turned into a museum, honoring the life and times of Sir William Mackenzie.

The original Mackenzie house was a large and rather plainly detailed mid-Victorian dwelling of two stories and an attic, but with an irregular outline. It is constructed of brick with projecting half-octagon front bays finished with gables, the center with a protective umbrage to a balcony above and the main entrance below, later filled in with glazing and a storm door. The ends project likewise and also have gables of high pitch with massive chimney stacks in an elaborate pilastered treatment. The bargeboard decoration to the verges is a solid detail resembling a carved form, but made, it would seem, from large-scale Victorian trim reminiscent of about 1890. Windows have segmental heads, decorated with a Victorian imitation of labels, the upper sash much divided, possibly an improvement about 1900. Additions continued behind the house in shingle-clad wings. The interior has largely the appearance of an Edwardian house.

D. MacDonald-Ross 1979

The Whiteside Homestead

LITTLE BRITAIN

What wealthy farmer dwells in view
Of Little Britain town
Who settled here in '42
What man of high renown
Its none of England's lords and peers,
Nor yet the Pope of Rome,
Nor yet the Day of proud Algiers;
Its R. F. Whiteside's home.

The home of Robert Ferguson Whiteside, built about 1850, presented a fascinating example of formal landscape of the period with a round flower bed encircled by a path leading to the front door. Lush gardens enclosed by a delicate picket fence reflected an attitude of pride in the home.

The story of Robert Whiteside begins in 1831, when at twenty-six years of age, he walked from Little Britain, Lancaster County, Pennsylvania, to Newmarket, Ontario. The journey took a month. Upon his arrival, he met David Ellerby, an Englishman and an experienced woolen merchant. In January, 1832, they entered a ten-year partnership in the woolen business.

In 1840 Robert and David purchased a mill about a mile above Holland Landing and began operation. By 1842 Robert sold his share of the business and moved to Mariposa with his wife Margaret and family. The journey took three days. The community was relatively new; the settlers were generally poor and had to struggle over the few rough roads on ox sleds all year round. During the busiest season the water supply needed to operate the mills was not dependable. The location was good, however, with excellent soil for farming.

Robert's comparative wealth and integrity earned him considerable prominence and esteem. Immediately be began construction on a dam to harness the water power and establish a grist and sawmill. Later he built a woolen factory. Until the post office was established, Robert called the village Elm Grove, but later discovered an Elm Grove post office elsewhere. At a meeting to select another name, he proposed Little Britain; someone else proposed Margareteville, after Margaret Whiteside; and a third person proposed Balsam Grove. Little Britain received the most votes and became the name of the village in 1854.

Being insatiably industrious, the Whitesides worked hard and their wealth steadily increased. About 1860 their estate was worth between fifteen and twenty thousand dollars, and the earnings of the mills were seven hundred to fourteen hundred a year. Robert generally had several hundred dollars lent out in small sums to men who required funds. When township councils were first established, he was elected to the council and served for many years.

The Whiteside Homestead burned to the ground in the early 1900s, but an old photograph of the house survived the flames, preserving the memory of its magnificence.

A formal elevation with center door flanked by a window has two windows above in this two-story house. The house appears to be transitional from the older and stricter vernacular to the early Victorian southern Ontario house. The doorcase is elaborate with pilaster trim, but the door is four-paneled. The eaves are sloped, hence the gable ends lack returns. The shutters, some half open, others fully closed, have rods operating louvered panels, a feature not common before the midcentury. Yet the encircling porch, with its slender columns chamfered and elliptically arched infilling, harks back to older tastes. The finish appears smooth and could have been stucco.

The Shaw Homestead

SEAGRAVE

Over one hundred years ago a small center known as Shaw's Community existed outside Seagrave, Ontario. The Shaws arrived from Ireland about 1830 and settled on two hundred acres of land. Thomas and John Shaw first built a log cabin and by 1846 had donated a portion of land across from them for a log schoolhouse, appropriately called Shaw's School. The schoolhouse later became a branch of the Methodist Church with Miss Sophia Shaw as a missionary collector. The Shaws continued to help build the community by providing more land for a cemetery near the school.

In 1863 all the neighbors gathered for a bee to raise the Shaw Church. When it was completed, the men walked across the road to help the Shaws raise their new frame house. On completion they took great pride in having participated in the building of one of the most stately homes in the countryside.

Certainly a stylish house, it was capped with a widow's walk surrounded with small paned windows. From the interior the windows were at eye level, providing a fine view in all directions.

Originally these observation decks were used by wives awaiting their husbands' return. Men often traveled on journeys that kept them away from home for a week or more. By day a wife could keep watch; at night she would light a coal oil lamp in the widow's walk as a guiding beacon for the returning traveler. If he failed to return, having met with an accident or been robbed and murdered, the wife, would pace the room atop the house awaiting her husband's return until she was notified that she was a widow. Thus the room received its name, widow's walk.

A bell erected on the back roof of the Shaw house was used to call the men in from the fields for meals, or for emergencies. The bell is still there but is seldom used today. Mississauga Indians of Scugog Island often canoed from their eight-hundred-acre reserve across the lake to Shaw land to trade, exchanging baskets for blankets and food.

Since no records were kept of the Shaw family, stories handed down from one owner of the Shaw homestead to the next provide the only link with their past. The schoolhouse no longer exists and the church was torn down in 1928. Thomas Shaw, his wife Charlotte, and their children lie buried in the Shaw cemetery.

The tall proportion of this two-story hipped-roof frame house is further emphasized by the center monitor or belvedere to the roof, but the low pitched hip roof helps to maintain a pleasant form. The house had end chimneys, one still serving a fireplace, the other stoves. It is a familiar three-bay design with a center doorway having eared trim in the Greek Revival mode framing a heavily fielded six-panel door, enclosed by simply divided side-lights and transom. A single-story kitchen wing extends to the rear.

Philippa Faulkner 79

The Bigelow House

PORT PERRY

Port Perry owes a great deal of its prosperity to one man, a visionary with practical purpose who would often ride roughshod over opposition. Joseph Bigelow was that man.

Born in 1828, he moved with his parents and nine brothers from Simcoe County to Lindsay in 1844. His father, Hiram Bigelow, started a successful flour-milling business there. Joseph and his twin, Joel, left Lindsay in 1851 for Port Perry, where they opened a general store under the name "J. & J. Bigelow." (Joel later moved on to Whitby and then Chicago for a distinguished career in real estate.) The next year Joseph became the first postmaster for Port Perry and continued to serve in this position until 1869. He married Elizabeth Paxton in 1854 and over the next eight years began to mold his dreams.

Joseph bought a woolen factory and planing mill and expanded the business to the manufacture of barrel staves. The factory operated until 1870, when the railway expropriated the land. A mill owned by a Stephen Doty failed and Joseph bought it out. When the Royal Canadian Bank opened a branch in Port Perry in 1862, Joseph Bigelow became manager, a position he held for six years.

After the building of a three-story commercial emporium called The Royal Arcade, Bigelow's next project was promoting the construction of the Port Whitby and Port Perry Railway.

The first council of Port Perry met in 1872 with Joseph Bigelow as its reeve, and he continued to serve in office until 1874. In 1877 he became a justice of the peace and the new owner of an elaborate Italianate house designed and built by H. R. Barber, of Oshawa. The interior was equally elaborate, with heavy trim, archways, and a grand staircase prominently placed in a generous hall. The summer kitchen was in the full-sized basement and the winter kitchen was situated at the rear of the house. The drawing room, reception room, dining room, and domestic offices were all on the first floor, with bedrooms and maids' quarters on the second. Joseph planned to build a number of fireplaces with marbleized slate mantelpieces throughout the house, but his wife refused to permit it, arguing that a fireplace dirtied rather than heated a home.

Joseph Bigelow failed by three votes to get elected to the Ontario Legislature in 1881, but this defeat did not stop him from continuing to promote and establish business in Port Perry.

When Joseph died in 1917 at the age of eighty-nine, flags flew at half-mast on public buildings in tribute to a man whose insight and spirit enabled him to make his dreams a reality. The Bigelow House still remains in the family and is now owned by Mr. and Mrs. William Carnegie of Port Perry.

It is not often that one sees a late Italianate house so complete and well preserved on the exterior. The iron cresting to the flat decks of the roof, tower, bay window, and entrance porch are still intact, and the generous eaves are still adorned with fanciful brackets. Even the verandah survives. In fact, only the chimneys have lost their ornamental caps to the weather and perhaps the roof covering has been replaced. This large residence exudes prestige, a family with wealth. Its white brick exterior, low-pitched gables, and elaborate outline and an extended ell with the angle punctuated with a dramatic tower hail it as the end of the mid-Victorian period, evolving from the influence of Andrew Jackson Downing and his partner, Calvert Vaux, who describes such houses in his book, Villages and Cottages, *published in New York in 1857.*

The Parr House and General Store

BLACKSTOCK

At one time any stranger coming to the hamlet of Blackstock could expect a bag of water to be dropped from the roof of the hotel onto his head. William Parr and Tom Swain, two local business-men, made a perfect team, pulling various tricks on the villagers. William Parr built and owned the general store in Blackstock, and Tom Swain owned the hotel just two doors away.

Parr built the store and a house adjacent to it in the late 1890s. He was a constant source of intrigue, a man about town whom everyone acknowledged whether they shared his odd sense of humor or not. One incident involved a man who purchased a pair of boots in Parr's store. The customer charged the merchandise to his account and left, but by the end of the day Parr had forgotten which customer it was, so he decided to charge every customer who came into the store that day for a pair of boots. Naturally each time the customers denied buying the boots, he believed them, and by the process of elimination he finally located the right person.

Parr and Swain were not the only village charac-ters. William Hooey was also well known for his blend of dry humor and ready wit. One time he accused the hotelkeeper in Blackstock of using his fence rails as firewood. The man denied the accusa-tion emphatically. Later that night Hooey bored a hole in one of his fence rails, filled it with gun-powder, and put in a plug. The next morning the stove in the sitting room of the hotel blew up.

In time Blackstock became a thriving commu-nity. In 1861 the first fall fair was held there and has continued to this day. During the winter people would gather together and go for sleigh rides. The first stop would be Tom Swain's hotel, where every-one would step in for a drink or two. During one of these stop-overs William Parr and a few friends tied the sleigh to a pole with logging chains. When everyone rushed out and climbed into the sleigh, the driver cracked the whip and the horses were off. Suddenly the sleigh stopped dead with a jolt and everyone spilled off.

When Parr married, he built a house with a verandah in front. It was of brick construction, with a simple plan featuring a parlor, dining room, summer kitchen, and pantry with a hallway leading into the store. Two bedrooms were located on the second floor with an entrance to two more bed-rooms over the store. Parr and his wife, Sophia McLaughlin, raised two sons and four daughters in this house. His son Herb eventually took over the store until it was sold in 1911.

The store and house changed hands many times until Bill and Sandy Thompson purchased the property in 1976. Not wishing to see another gen-eral store disappear, Bill decided to continue the business. Although the verandah on the house is enclosed now and the store verandah has been destroyed, Bill and Sandy hope to replace it some-day. In the meantime they are busy restoring the interior of their home.

The Parr Homestead is a store with attached resi-dence, the store section projecting forward to the street. The roof is a steeply pitched gable over a story and a half. The store wing is a low-pitched form with the hipped gable facing the street. The building appears to be frame, the north side clad in cove siding. Other faces are veneered in patterned brick, white or buff brick being used for quoins and ornamental window heads representing label out-lines further elaborated by a keystone effect at the center. Window heads are segmental generally, but a round-arched opening occurs in the front gable to the house. The house entrance is slightly off-center; the door is glazed above, with heavy bolection molds to panels below. The arc above the door is filled by a panel having incised decoration. The shopfront is relatively modern, but the other win-dows to the building are a characteristic later Victorian pattern of four panes.

Frederick Graham's Homestead

PRINCE ALBERT

Recently, while I was standing between two brothers looking over their two hundred acres, one said, "You know, my brother and I could sell out tomorrow and never worry about money again. We could travel to Las Vegas with our pockets full, but what would that leave our families?"

The property they spoke of was Christie land, located in Prince Albert, Ontario, and first purchased by Reuben Crandell in 1821. When Alexander and Frederick Graham arrived in Prince Albert from Kircud-bright-shire, Scotland, in 1842, they purchased this property and divided it into two one-hundred-acre parcels. Both brothers built homes for themselves, Frederick's being constructed in 1850 with local Scottish stone masons doing the work.

The bricks for the house were produced from the second field south of the house. The eight-room dwelling was built on a formal plan, with a hall flanked by a bedroom and winter kitchen on the left and a parlor and parlor bedroom to the right. A back kitchen, with a porch and woodshed, was at the rear of the house.

The center staircase with pine railing led to the four bedrooms upstairs. The large hearth in the winter kitchen warmed the front bedroom, while a fireplace in the parlor kept the frost from the parlor bedroom.

Frederick did not marry, and when he died in 1877 he willed the house to his brother's daughter, Mary Honor Graham, with the provision that she cared for her uncles, William and James. She honored the will and took care of both men in her father's house.

When Uncle William arrived in Prince Albert he was destitute after investing all his money in the Confederacy and losing two sons who fought for the South during the American Civil War. He died a year later. James lived much longer, often lying in his bed upstairs and pounding on the floor with his cane when he wanted attention.

Mary decided to rent her uncle's house to William Pearson and his family, preferring to remain in her father's home even after she had wed Peter Christie. Finally, in 1920, Mary and Peter moved into Frederick Graham's house and gave the other home to their son Grant and his wife.

Eventually Mary's other son, Graham, inherited the house. Residing in Maryland, his family used it as a summer home until his daughter Catharine Christie moved there in 1955. Catharine sold the homestead in 1977 to Patricia and Ralph Price of Prince Albert. Generally the appearance of the homestead has changed very little, with the interior remaining intact. The only significant change has been the rearrangement of the back kitchen and woodshed.

This story-and-a-half red brick house, with its low-pitched gable roof, eaves returns, and chimneys, typifies the local building in the Classical tradition, the vernacular of southern Ontario in the first half of the 19th century. The three-bay front with semi-elliptical head to the center doorway, fanlight, and sidelights are also typical. But here there is no elaborate Flemish bond brickwork to the principal façade, and the combination of red and white brick in the chimney stacks, together with a certain exaggerated breadth in the cornices, suggests a date closer to the mid-century.

Cedar Cliff

BROOKLIN

Among the first to settle in Brooklin, Ontario, was John Campbell. In 1832 he purchased several hundred acres where a section of Brooklin now stands. Never a man to let grass grow under his feet, Campbell had men chop and clear land and within a year had planted one hundred acres of fall wheat. From this start the village of Brooklin began and by 1851 its population had reached five hundred and fifty.

Stephen Mede Thomas arrived in Brooklin in the late 1850s with his four brothers. Four years later he purchased land and began construction of his house. A grand edifice, appearing as a massive gingerbread house surrounded by towering fir trees, it was one of Brooklin's largest residences. After planting a row of cedars on either side of the walkway leading to the house, Stephen named his new home Cedar Cliff. Sitting on a small knoll with a creek meandering beside it, the house overlooked the main street. Shortly after its completion he built a two-story brick general store north of the creek on the west side, immediately south of the house.

In 1872 Thomas turned ten acres of land on Concession 5 into Graveside Cemetery, with plots laid out and ready for use in the spring of 1874. Ironically, the first person buried there was Nancy Hault, the undertaker's wife.

By 1881 Stephen Thomas had sold Cedar Cliff to Richard Moore for thirty-five hundred dollars and moved to the United States. An announcement of his death in Dover, Delaware, appeared in the Whitby *Chronicle* of June 18, 1897. Cedar Cliff changed ownership nine times until James and Wilma Carnwith purchased it in 1948 for twenty-three thousand dollars. The Carnwith family has taken great pride in Cedar Cliff and the house continues to be surrounded by beautiful gardens and stands as a reminder to Brooklin of its unique history.

Cedar Cliff is a romantic Gothic Revival house with the elaborate outline so often favored to display the picturesque adornment of the period. Here the "Gothique" leans toward the Tudor with labels or heavy hood molds around the heads of openings and the twin circular shafts to the gable and chimney. The house is basically a T-shaped plan with a rear wing, the whole of two stories with steeply pitched gable roofs providing attics. The front of the house, facing roughly south, has a projecting bay with a small doorway to the encircling verandah, but the main entrance with transom and sidelights is on one side at the end of the house closest to the street. The main gables are richly ornamented with bargeboards in a looped die design, finials at the peaks and acorn pendants or drops at the lower corners, the bargeboards continuing in a fretted wave pattern along the eaves.

The James House

UXBRIDGE

The trail of James and Janet James from Wales to Pennsylvania in 1684 ended in the murder of James in Upper Canada.

Ezekial James, a Quaker, left Pennsylvania in 1803 with his wife Hezeah and their seven children in pursuit of a new life in eastern Ontario. They settled in Whitechurch Township near Toronto, an event that marked the beginning of the Quaker movement in Ontario. In 1805 Ezekiel, Jr., aged twenty-three, and his wife Ruth moved east to the Township of Uxbridge, where they purchased two hundred acres. Ezekiel built a two-story fieldstone house a half-mile from the concession road and a quarter of a mile from the Uxbridge Settlement trail. The building was typical of early houses, with a back kitchen, a woodshed at right angles, and a driving house with a breezeway between. The family could reach the outhouse by way of this breezeway. A beam was built into the stonework of the house to accommodate an attaching one-story verandah.

In 1828 Ezekiel James hired John Christie to help him through the harvest. Ezekiel agreed, as part of the compensation, to move Christie and his family to York at the end of the season. When the time came to move them, Ezekiel was ill and his eldest son, Isaac, took his place behind his father's fine span of dapple-gray mares. Isaac had never made the four-day round trip journey to York before. He wanted to take a gun in case they saw some game in the fourteen miles of woods, but Christie persuaded him not to do so, saying he had pistols and plenty of ammunition.

Twice that night Mrs. James dreamed that she saw her son wounded, groaning in agony. When Isaac did not return as expected on the fifth day, Mrs. James and her son John, a lad of fifteen, saddled two horses and set out, looking carefully into every thicket and swamp along the road. They finally reached her brother, Isaac Lundy, at Whitechurch without finding anything suspicious.

No one had seen the team pass by and the alarm immediately went out to a blacksmith's shop on Yonge Street, where the horses had frequently been shod. The blacksmith reported that he had seen the team pass with a stranger driving, but he had seen nothing of Isaac. That night Mrs. James heard a voice bidding her to search "in the woods" and the next day she led a party about a mile into the woods. She stopped, pointed to a log heap on the right-hand side of the road and told the men to search there. In a matter of minutes Isaac was discovered. He had been clubbed and shot thorough the head.

Christie was charged with wilful murder and the government of Upper Canada issued a proclamation offering a reward of one hundred pounds for his arrest. When apprehended in New York State less than a week after the murder, he confessed to the crime and was sentenced to be hanged. He was executed on Thursday, October 30, 1828, and his body was dissected and anatomized. It has been said that a neighbor of Ezekial James went to visit a doctor in Toronto, and upon entering his office was met by the doctor, who pointed to a skeleton in the corner and said, "You remember John Christie."

The James House is of fieldstone, two-stories and an attic high, the low-pitched gable roof with prominent but thin eaves returns. The cornice is strange, without a frieze and only cove and beveled bedmould from wall to soffit. The house had end chimneys, originally serving fireplaces on the ground floor, as large crumbling bases in the cellar indicate. A later one-story kitchen wing, finished in stucco, has been added to the west near the north end. The three-bay front faces west, and had a simple center doorway with a four-panel door, the windows above with sash of eight panes over eight, those below originally with twelve over eight. The north gable end had three windows to the ground floor, one converted to a door, and two above, the south gable three windows to both floors, not quite symmetrically spaced in either case.

The Lowrie Homestead

SCOTT TOWNSHIP

Overlooking a flowering meadow lit with vibrant colors stands the Lowrie Homestead. Built by Robert Lowrie in the 1860s, this hewn log house is humble in size, measuring twenty by twenty-six feet, yet it creates an aura of warmth and comfort. The dark stained logs, some measuring two feet in width, blend into a setting of tanned wheat fields and the Black River meandering past in the distance.

Originally the house featured one large room on the first floor with a stairway leading to one room on the second. A winter kitchen was housed in the back of the building, joined by a summer kitchen and a woodshed. Two small bedrooms added onto the first floor at a later date. The interior walls were decorated with horsehair plaster in 1886.

Robert Lowrie was born in Scotland and when he was two his parents emigrated to Canada. He lived in Vaughan Township until he married and moved to Scott Township, where he purchased land ten miles north of Uxbridge on Lot 25, Concession 5, and built his home. Just a short distance from the log house is a foundation of a cabin, indicating that he had built a temporary dwelling to live in until his house was completed.

In February of 1872 the house appeared for sale in the *Uxbridge Journal*. The advertisement read: "Farm for sale—will be sold subject to a mortgage of $960.00, a valuable farm of 100 acres, 60 cleared, the balance of 40 acres well-wooded with hardwood and cedar, and well fenced. On the premises are a hewn log dwelling with a good stone cellar, and frame barn."

Why Robert would wish to sell his farm so soon after building it is unknown. The advertisement continued to appear several times during the 1870s, but no one bought the property. Eventually his brother James became the owner and the farm remained in the Lowrie family until 1965, still without hydro or running water.

Chris and Jan Wrong purchased the farm in 1967 and began renovations on the house and barn. Rooms were added to the house and water and electricity installed. The cedar shingle roof on the barn was replaced with tin and the fences mended around the fields.

The appearance of the farm has changed very little over the years. The roof may still leak a little and the winter kitchen still has no heat, but the natural pioneering spirit continues to live on.

This small log house, actually of flattened or hewn timber slabs, is characteristic of the early architecture in the once-forested areas of southern Ontario. The timber selected was generally the native white pine, attaining in virgin woodland statuesque proportions and a clear, straight trunk easily fashioned with a broad-ax. The projecting porch or "pent" roof is most commonly associated with log construction where the beams of the second floor project to provide a support for the outer ends of the roof. The walls are chinked with lime mortar. The gable end of the low-pitched roof is framed with studs and finished in horizontal clapboard.

Allan McGillivray '79

Tepee

BLACK RIVER

By 1850 Upper Canada was no longer wilderness. Old trails had become roads and fur trading gave way to farming. Inevitably, the original inhabitants retreated into the shadows.

Richard Cornelius, an Oneida Indian, was born that same year. His tribe belonged to the Iroquois Confederation, which once inhabited the region east of Lake Ontario, just south of the St. Lawrence River. As a young brave Richard ventured into the Uxbridge area and settled there at the mouth of Black River.

He clung to the old ways of his forefathers, building himself a skin tepee measuring between fourteen and sixteen feet. The structure was covered with summer-killed hides because they were thinner and lighter in weight. He anchored the tepee tightly by cutting holes around the lower edge of the hide and driving pegs through. Smoke flaps were then crossed over in front to the smoke vent and completely closed. A fire inside allowed the smoke to permeate the entire hide cover, helping to waterproof the structure and preventing the skin from becoming hard and stiff following a wetting.

The outward appearance of a tepee varied from tribe to tribe. Many used a foundation of three poles forming a tripod; others had a foundation of four poles. A principal attribute of the tepee was the open fire in the center with a smoke vent directly above. If the tepee was a true cone, the vent would be located around the crossing of the poles at the apex. In order to allow for proper ventilation without having a gaping hole at the top, the Indians would tilt the tepee and extend the smoke hole down the long side at the front of the tent. The crossing of poles was at the top end of the smoke hole instead of the middle, allowing projecting flaps to close over the hole. When new, a tepee is pure white; it later changes to a cream color. As it ages the top begins to darken from the constant smoke rising out the vent. Cornelius's home certainly exemplified a beauty of form and line.

He survived by trapping for a living, snagging muskrat, mink, and raccoon and selling the pelts to merchants in York. He never forgot the old customs taught to him by his people, and became known for his Indian medicine. Many settlers traveled to him to purchase his brewed bark and roots to cure their ailments. One of his popular remedies was wild ginseng, a herb with legendary attributes for curing back and stomach aches and for stimulating the body to perform better under stress.

On a winter's day in 1940 Cornelius, then ninety years old, was traveling in a car with three other men when they collided with a milk truck. Cornelius, another passenger, and the truck driver were killed. He was buried in the Uxbridge cemetery. Today nothing remains of his encampment; nor does any marker show his burial site. Only a few elderly residents remember the Oneida Indian who in the twentieth century lived the way his forefathers had.

The tepee is associated in most people's minds with the traditional shelter of the largely nomadic aboriginal tribes of North America, but this was by no means universal. Economical in its cone-shaped form, and easily demounted, transported, and re-erected, it was obviously shelter for a tougher breed.

Laurel Campbell-Stark '79 ©

Notes on Artists

George Balbar was born in Regina, Saskatchewan. Mainly a self-taught artist, he has had ten one-man shows and was included in Toronto's Art Gallery of Ontario traveling watercolor show in 1975-76. The following year his work was shown in the Japanese-Canadian watercolor exchange show and subsequent tours in Japan and Canada. He is a member of the Canadian Society of Watercolour Artists; and his work is now represented in private and public collections across Canada. Mr. Balbar is head of advertising for Simpson-Sears in St. Catharines, where he resides with his family. His drawings appear on pages 7 and 17.

Richard D. Brown was born, raised, and educated in Toronto. After graduating from the Ontario Colllege of Art in 1953, he settled down to advertising agency life. "Old Toronto" was the subject of his first one-man show, held at the Aggregation Gallery in Toronto. He was later commissioned by the Canadian National Railways Historical Division to sketch a series of railroad stations from Newfoundland to British Columbia, and then railway business cars and old steam locomotives. His drawings appear on pages 21 and 55.

Jane Buckles was born in Toronto in 1941. She graduated from the University of Toronto, Fine Arts, in 1964 and then attended the Ontario College of Education. She taught art at the secondary school level for several years before concentrating on her own work. Mainly known for her large stitched figures, Jane has shown in various galleries in Toronto and Montreal. Her work is included in collections throughout Canada and the United States. Jane now resides in Uxbridge, Ontario. Her drawing appears on page 113.

Gary Burns has a particular interest in architecture, which led to a study of architectural developments in Brantford. The study resulted in guest lectures for the Art Gallery of Brant and leading tours for the Brant County branch of the Architectural Conservancy of Ontario. Gary currently resides in Brantford. His drawing appears on page 35.

Laurel Campbell-Stark was born in Toronto in 1951. She graduated from the Ontario College of Art, majoring in drawing and painting. She continued her studies at Carlton University, Ottawa, and Ryerson Polytechnical Institute, Toronto. She has participated in group shows and juried exhibitions since 1978 and is now a freelance illustrator and designer. Her work is found in private and public collections in Canada. Recently published works include the 1979 Durham Regional Calendar and the 1979 Cannington Centennial Calendar. Laurel lives in Oshawa and is represented by the Margot Samuel Gallery in that city. Her drawings appear on pages 3, 97, 109, and 121.

Thomas Dean Coucill was born April 25, 1952, in Toronto. He majored in architecture during high school and later studied art and design at the Ontario College of Art. His work has been exhibited in Various Toronto galleries. Many of his drawings and paintings can also be found in Canadian homes and offices. His drawings appear on pages 57, 59, and 61.

Walter J. Coucill was born in June 22, 1915, at Camden, New Jersey, of English parentage. He attended school in England, then came to Canada with his parents in 1924 and has lived in Toronto since then. In his youth he lived in a log cabin in northern Ontario and made many canoe trips throughout Ontario. He attended Scarborough High School, Danforth Technical School, and Ontario College of Art. He has been an art director for Exhibition and Display Design, a member of the Royal Canadian Air Force, latterly as art director for the official RCAF magazine *Wings*. He is a member of the Royal Canadian Academy of Arts and his work is represented in public and private collections across Canada. His drawing appears on page 63.

Gordon R. Couling is a native of Guelph. He has been active as an artist, teacher, and writer. For twenty-five years Professor Couling was a member of the faculty of the University of Guelph and served as the first chairman of its Department of Fine Arts. His drawings appear on pages 45, 47, and 49.

Gayle Crosmaz is a resident of Castleton, Ontario. She studied during the summer of 1978 at the Schneider School of Fine Arts in Toronto. She was selected in three juried exhibitions, 1978-79: two years consecutively at the Cobourg Art Gallery, two drawings for the East Central Ontario Art Association, and a purchase award by the Ontario Society of Artists. Gayle's work is now represented in the Bagnani Art Collection. Her drawings appear on pages 79, 81, and 83.

Janice A. Croston was born in Wallasey, England, in 1958 and now resides in Scarborough, Ontario. She will be completing her final year of Graphic Design in May of 1980 at Durham College of Applied Arts and Technology in Oshawa. Her drawing appears on page 69.

Joan-Marie Dean was born in Ottawa, Ontario, and received an honors degree in Fine Arts from the University of Toronto. Her work has been included in many juried exhibitions and has been shown in solo exhibitions in Port Hope, Oshawa, Whitby, Toronto, and Ottawa. Her studio is in Oshawa, where she has resided with her husband and three children since 1967. She has been active in the Creative Artists In-Schools program through the Ontario Arts Council, and has work in many permanent and private collections. Her drawings appear on pages 71 and 73.

George Elliot is a creative specialist in commercial art with the Outboard Marina Corporation in Peterborough. He also teaches various art classes in the Continuing Education Program at Sir Sanford Fleming College in Lindsay. His work is sold mainly through the Art Loft Gallery in Peterborough. His drawing appears on page 99.

Philippa Faulkner is a graduate of Parsons College, New York, and now lives in Toronto. She has studied with Hans Hofmann, Varley, and Pinto and has worked as an assistant to Carl Schaeffer at the Schneider School of Fine Arts in Toronto. She spent some time on a scholarship studying art at the Instituto Allende in Mexico, and in 1968 received an international first award in Acapulco. Her work is represented in collections at the Art Gallery of Hamilton, Xerox of Canada, Royal Trust Company, and Hammond International. Her drawings appear on pages 107 and 115.

John Gibson who lives in Hagersville, Ontario, is a seventeen-year-old Indian artist of the Six Nations Mohawk tribe. His art has been exhibited at the Sheraton Centre in Toronto and the Brantford Cultural Centre. In his spare time John works on various cartoon strips, which have been printed in the Dundas *Star Weekly* newspaper. His drawing appears on page 33.

Lindsey Hallam is an illustrator, stage designer, and painter who lives in a big stone house in the country southwest of Toronto. She has won awards for her paintings and theater designs, has published a children's

book, and believes in magic and elves. Her drawings appear on pages 87 and 89.

John Hanson is a native of Hamilton, Ontario, and has studied at the Hamilton Technical Institute and the Institute of Art in Westport, Conn. He has won in both fine arts and commercial awards, and his work is represented in permanent and private collections in Canada, United States, Great Britain, and Bermuda. His drawings appear on pages 23, 25, 27, 29, and 31.

Paul Johns was born and educated in Toronto and currently lives in St. Catharines, Onatrio. As an employee of Simpson-Sears for twenty-eight years in Toronto and Montreal, he worked in various capacities: display-interior decorating, advertising, and store planning. As a designer he has been employed by hotels, restaurants, and colleges and has decorated residences in Toronto, Montreal, Miami, and Rio de Janeiro. Upon retiring he moved to Niagara-on-the-Lake and restored and designed several houses there. He is a past president of the Niagara Historical Society and has taught for the last eight years at Niagara College of Applied Arts and Technology, teaching history of Architecture, drawing, design, and renderings in various mediums. His drawings appear on pages 9, 11, and 13.

Donald MacDonald-Ross is the son of an Irish artist. He has found the beautiful homes of Ontario an outlet for his love and appreciation of our Canadian heritage. He and his family live in Kirkfield in Sir William Mackenzie's historic home, where they are all busily engaged in turning back the clock to showcase the life and times of Sir William Mackenzie. His drawing of the house appears on page 103.

Les Maund has resided in the St. Catharines area for

all of his thirty years, and has always been fascinated by the historic buildings in the area. It was not until 1972, however, that he put his self-taught talent to work in earnest and began doing pen-and-ink sketches for his own enjoyment and that of his family and friends. Since that time he has successfully exhibited his art throughout the Niagara area and has done several pen-and-ink series of hasty notes for local publishers. Les now operates Stirling Graphics in St. Catharines and continues to sketch the Niagara Peninsula. His drawings appear on pages 5, 15, and 19.

Janet McGhee was born in Oshawa, Ontario, where she now resides. For the past seven years she has instructed watercolor classes and recently conducted a series of painting field trips for the Robert McLaughlin Gallery. Her work is found in private, corporate, and public collections across Canada and in the United States and Europe. Her drawings appear on pages 91, 93, and 95.

Allan McGillivray is a teacher-artist-historian who lives in Zephyr, Ontario, where he is converting a century-old church building into a studio-home called Winnowing Studio. He does local landscapes in oils and ink sketches of historic buildings. His drawings appear on pages 117 and 119.

Kathryn McHolm works "on the spot" and enjoys all the surrounding distractions when creating her watercolor and pen-and-ink works. Flowers, quilts, and architectural features have supplied inspiration for the number of shows that have taken place over the last four years. Her work can be viewed at her shop the Bric-a-Brac Shack in Port Hope. Her drawings appear on pages 75 and 77.

Phil McLorn   was born in China and came to St. Thomas, Ontario, in 1947. He studied advertising design at the Ontario College of Art in Toronto and graduated in 1957. His watercolors carry a definite element of design in composition and color. He is married to Devona Paquette and they reside in Ayr, Ontario. His drawing appears on pages 37 and 41.

Sean Kilpatrick McQuay   was born December 20, 1956, was raised on a farm in Whitby, Ontario, by a Glaswegian mother and a Canadian father. He is an artist-writer whose work paces the border between utter nonsense and extreme seriousness. He has traveled extensively throughout Britain and Europe and is happy to wander and draw and draw and write and write and wander. He worked at the Robert McLaughlin Gallery, Oshawa, on and off for the past three years, and is now attending the Nova Scotia College of Art and Design in Halifax. His drawing of the McQuay house appears on page 67.

Brenda Milner   studied at the College of Art, Manchester, specializing in textile design. She traveled widely, designing and selling mainly for the silk-screen market. She worked for a time in an engineering office as a tracer-draftswoman. Since living in Canada she has done pen-and-ink illustrations for books and hasty notes, as well as many landscapes, flower paintings and buildings in watercolor. Brenda is married, has two

grown children, and resides in Lindsay, where she teaches basic drawing techniques and watercolour in the Continuing Education Program at Sir Sanford Fleming College. She has had two very successful solo exhibitions of her work, and is working toward her next show in 1980. Her drawings appear on pages 101 and 105.

Kenneth G. Montgomery   was born and educated in Toronto, and is a production planning manager with the Steel Company of Canada. He began to paint in 1964, after moving to Burlington, where he studied with Gerry Puley, Gordon Perrier, and Philip Sybol. Ken is currently working in pen-and-ink and acrylics. He has exhibited in the C.K.O.C. Show in Hamilton and, for the past few years, in the Bruce Trail Calendar. His drawings appear on pages 51 and 53.

Devona Paquette   was born in Woodstock, Ontario. She studied general design at the Ontario College of Art and graduated in 1955. She has won a reputation for her exuberant watercolors and her life studies. She works out of her studio in Ayr, Ontario. Her drawings appear on pages 39 and 43.

John E. Secord   was born in London, Ontario, and graduated from the Ontario College of Art, where he won a drawing scholarship. Throughout his extensive career in advertising, he painted and sketched in Mexico, England, Portugal, Greece, Italy, Bermuda and the

West Indies, as well as many parts of Canada. He now lives in Toronto, where he devotes his full time to art. John has had nine one-man shows over the past eight years. His drawing appears on page 65.

Sandra Thompson   was born and raised in Port Perry, Ontario. She received an Honors Bachelor of Fine Arts degree from York University and a Bachelor of Education degree from the University of Toronto (Faculty of Education). She now teaches art at I. E. Weldon Secondary School in Lindsay. Sandra and her husband Bill reside in Blackstock, Ontario. Her drawing appears on page 111.

Ronald P. Thurston   was born and educated in Meaford, Ontario, and graduated in engineering from the University of Toronto. He began painting seriously in 1967 in Burlington while studying under Gerry Puley. An active member of the Burlington Fine Arts Association, he also studied portraiture, watercolors, life drawing, and print-making at the Dundas Valley School of Art. He compiled, edited, and administered the Bruce Trail Calendar of original artwork for six years before moving to Cobourg in 1976. In Cobourg he continued with his artistic interests as an active member of the Cobourg Art Gallery, a National Exhibition Centre in historic Victoria Hall. Ron's work is represented in many private collections in Toronto, Hamilton, Burlington, and Cobourg, as well as western Canada. His drawing appears on page 85.

Glossary of Architectural Terms

Ashlar: squared, cut, or hewn stone with a smoothly dressed face, often as a veneer to a rubble or brick wall.

Balustrade: a low screen comprising balusters, or turnings supporting a coping or handrail; by extension the handrail assembly to a stair including balusters, newels, and scroll with baluster cage if such is part of the design.

Bargeboard: the ornamental board, often *fretted,* hanging from the edge of the projecting *gable* roof or *verge* of Gothic Revival buildings, sometimes referred to as a vergeboard.

Bay: (1) a compartment or division of a façade indicated by an opening.
(2) a projection, such as a bay window.

Bedmould: the molding of a cornice immediately below the horizontal *soffit* and at the top of the vertical *frieze.*

Belvedere: a rooftop light, similar to a lantern, from which a good view could be obtained; this feature also served to light a loft or attic.

Board and batten: vertical boarding with narrow strips or battens, sometimes shaped or molded, applied over the joints and often associated with the cottage ornee in the Gothic Revival.

Bolection mold: panel molding, usually of bold scale, projecting beyond the surface of the door or paneling to create a rich effect.

Boomtown front: a false front, often to create the impression of a grander building or a formal façade to the street and masking the roof behind.

Box shutters: interior shutters, usually paneled, set in the splayed *reveals* of deep-set windows found in masonry buildings.

Bracket: a member to carry a horizontal projection, often used decoratively in cornices where it assumed

increasing elaboration as the Victorian period advanced.

Broached shape: resembling the transition from a gentle slope to a steep pitch and similar to a steeple emerging from the roof of a tower.

Casement sash: window lights hinged at the sides, usually to open in.

Chairrail: a rail set on the interior walls to correspond with the back of a straight chair in order to prevent damage to plaster surfaces and decoration.

Chamfered: beveled on the corners at 45°, and in a post often to form an octagon shape.

Clapboard: overlapping thin wood weatherboarding applied horizontally as the finish to a frame house.

Cleats: horizontal wood stiffeners secured to the back of vertical board doors; (by similar definition the strips nailed to walls or cupboards to support shelves).

Common bond: in brickwork, a pattern comprising several rows or courses of "stretchers" (bricks laid lengthwise) to a course of "headers" (or bricks laid on end).

Cornice: the decorative termination to a wall, the transition between wall and roof or, internally between wall and ceiling.

Cresting: vertical projecting ornamentation, usually of cast iron, similar to a low fence, decorating the tops of bay windows, porches, decks and ridges of roofs and towers in Victorian houses.

Cyma reversa: molding that has the concave part nearest the wall.

Dentil: a toothlike rectangular block set close together to form a row, usually below the *bedmould* of a cornice.

Doddy House: the addition made to a Mennonite

house to accommodate the retiring generation on the farm.

Dogtooth ornament: a chevron or triangular molding repeated to form an ornamental band, found on Gothic and Romanesque Revival work and derived from Early English and Norman.

Dormers: small windows projecting from the roof of a house to light the upper story, which usually contain bedrooms or sleeping space.

Dovetailed: a flared or fan-shaped joint, similar in outline to a dove's tail, used to provide a secure corner to log buildings (and also used in furniture, such as chests or drawers).

Drop: in the context used, a pendant or downward projecting ornament at the bottom of a *bargeboard,* and at the peak or ridge usually combined with a *finial.*

Eared trim: an outline of moldings forming a wide projecting headpiece which overlaps the side pieces slightly, much as the projecting ends of a lintel, popular in the Greek Revival style.

Eaves: the lower horizontal termination of a sloping roof, often projecting beyond the wall to form a *cornice.*

Eaves returns: the small horizontal extension of the eaves at the gable end of the house, often called "birdhouses" by carpenters because of their adopted function as a nesting site.

Eyebrow windows: a low *dormer* for light or ventilation on the slope of a roof, the roofing carried over it in a continuous wave line.

Fanlight: a round or semi-elliptical light, usually over a doorway, with a pattern of radiating *muntins* representing the ribs of a fan.

Fielded: with the center of the panel, such as that in a door, raised; hence: Fielding: the effect of the raised panel center.

Fieldstone: stone, usually taken from near the surface of a field, such as erratic granite boulders, and occasionally limestone, the former usually split and laid with smooth split faces to form the outer surface of the wall.

Finial: the upward projecting ornament at the peak of a gable usually associated with *bargeboards* and the Gothic Revival style.

Flat arch: an arch with splayed ends and bricks laid on edge to form a horizontal head to a wall opening.

Flemish bond: in brickwork, a pattern formed of alternating "stretchers" (bricks laid lengthwise) and "headers" (bricks laid on end) horizontally and vertically; hence: Flemish course: a course of stretchers alternating with headers.

Flushboarding: tight weatherboarding, fitted to form a flush surface, and usually applied horizontally, the boards tongued and often beaded at the upper edge and grooved at the lower edge.

French windows: windows, often with a lower solid wood panel, to the floor, and hinged at the sides; in effect, glazed doors.

Fretted ornament: a board with ornamental cut-out form, sometimes in wave effect or arabesque shapes; hence: Fretwork: fretted or cut-out ornament.

Frieze: the vertical portion, often richly ornamented, of an entablative at the top of wall and immediately below the *cornice.*

Gable: the triangular end well extension to fit the underside of a sloping roof; hence: Gable roof: a roof with front and back slopes only.

Gothic: pertaining to a style of architecture prevalent in western Europe from the 12th through the 15th centuries, characterized by pointed arches, rib vaulting, and flying buttresses.

Hip or hipped roof: a roof sloped on all four sides, sometimes referred to as a "cottage roof."

Hood mold: the projecting ornamental moldings over a wall opening which extend at the sides slightly below the head and then return outwards: also known as a *label.*

Ionic order: one of the classical Greek orders in architecture, characterized by a capital with two volutes or ram's-horn terminations at the corners.

Keystone: the center voussoir or wedge-shaped stone of an arch.

Label: a *hood mold,* characteristic of the Gothic Revival and imitated in later Victorian building.

Lintel: the beam, of stone or wood, over a wall opening.

Lunate windows: crescent-shaped ornamental windows, often seen in late Victorian and Edwardian villas.

Mansard roof: a curbed roof or hipped roof of double pitch, the lower section with a steep slope, the upper a flatter pitch and often in the late Victorian period a flat deck, named after the French Renaissance architect, Mansart.

Modillion cornice: a cornice with flat horizontal corbels, or console brackets, set relatively close together to ornament the *soffit.*

Monitor: a large roof light illuminating an attic or loft; the windows arranged around the vertical projection in the center of a *hipped roof.*

Mullion: the vertical dividing member between the lights of a window or separating a door from sidelights.

Muntin: the thin wood glazing bar dividing a window sash into glass panes.

Ogee: a double or reverse curve, the classical molding profile known as a *cyma reversa,* the outline often combined to form a sharply pointed head to an opening, essentially of the Gothic Revival.

Paling fence: a fence comprising vertical narrow boards, sometimes with ornamentally shaped tops, nailed relatively close together.

Parapet: the vertical extension of a wall concealing the roof behind.

Pediment: the triangular termination to a gable enclosed by the horizontal and raking cornices.

Pendant: a *drop* or ornamental downward projecting ornament to a *bargeboard* or *finial.*

Picket fence: a fence comprising slender square vertical wood pieces, usually let into the horizontal rails, the top of the pickets commonly pointed.

Pilaster: a flat, rectangular pier projecting slightly from the face of a wall.

Plinth: a projecting base, usually formed by the foundation of a house.

Porte-cochère: a porch through which vehicles may be driven and usually attached to the entrance of a house, (but originally in French an entrance wide enough to accommodate wheeled vehicles).

Quatrefoil: a cusped ornament of four lobes, resembling a four-leafed clover, a Gothic Revival detail.

Quoins: the accentuated members of a corner, often formed of stone, but also fashioned of brick and sometimes imitated in wood with alternating short and long pieces appearing to bond the corners of a building.

Rendering: an applied surface, usually of stucco.

Returns: see *eaves return:* the extension of the horizontal *eaves* at the *gable* end of a house.

Reveals: the sides and head of a recessed opening between the face of the wall and the window or door frame.

Roughcast: a stucco rendering of rough texture formed by lime-encrusted rounded gravel of small size and applied as a wet mixture dashed against the walls.

Rusticated quoins: *quoins* with deep V-joints between and sometimes with a rough surface emphasizing the boldness of the detail and often creating a more massive scale.

Scraffito: a design in incised outline.

Sidehill (position):   a bank location providing entrances from grade to two floors, usually the main floor and the story beneath.

Sidelight: the small light beside a door or on either side of the larger central light of a *Venetian* or *Wyatt window.*

Soffit: the horizontal lower surface of the projecting section of a *cornice.*

Spindles (spindlework):   short fine wood turnings often combined in decorative frieze or band assemblies to porches and interior screens of the late Victorian period.

Spoolwork: similar to *spindlework* but generally of shorter, squat turnings similarly repeated.

Stoop: the platform and accompanying steps in front of an entrance and a term often associated with the floor or whole of a porch or verandah.

Stretcher bond: in brickwork, a pattern comprising entirely stretchers; that is, bricks laid lengthwise.

String course: a continuous projecting band, often demarcating the floors of a building and occasionally coinciding with windowsills, when it is known as a sill course.

Transom: the rectangular member and sash above a door or window; hence: Transom bar: the horizontal bar below the sash and
Transom light: the sash of the transom.

Trellis: a screenwork of filigree design, often in elaborate patterns of chinoiserie in narrow panels supporting a porch or verandah roof; hence: Trellis post: a panel support of this order and
Trellis verandah: a verandah with trellis supports and often with a bowed or pagoda-like roof.

Tudor label: see *label* or *hood mold,* a projecting molding at the head of an opening associated with the Gothic Revival and is inspired by those of the Tudor period.

Tympanum: the space between the horizontal and raking cornices of a pediment.

Umbrage: a recess formed by building projections on either side and above.

Venetian window: in this context, a wide square-headed window divided into three sections by *mullions* usually with a wider center light and narrow *sidelights.*

Verge: the projection or edge of the roof at a *gable.*

Wyatt window: a *Venetian window* and favored by James Wyatt, the architect, in his work around the later 18th and early 19th centuries.

Bibliography

ADAMSON, ANTHONY, and MACRAE, MARION. *The Ancestral Roof: Domestic Architecture of Upper Canada.* Toronto: Clarke, Irwin and Company Limited, 1963.

Annals of the Forty: Loyalist's Pioneer Families of Lincoln 1783-1833. The Grimsby Historical Society, 1954. Volumes 5 and 6.

BROWN, GEORGE, HARMAN, ELEANOR, and JEANNERET, MARSH. *Canada in North America 1800-1901.* Toronto: Copp Clark Publishing Company Limited, 1961.

CONANT, THOMAS. *Life in Canada.* Toronto: William Briggs, 1903.

_____. *Upper Canada Sketches.* Toronto: William Briggs, 1898.

DENNIS, LLOYD, and FIELD, JOHN. *Land of Promise.* Toronto: The House of Grant (Canada), Ltd., 1960.

FARMER, SAMUEL. *On the Shores of Scugog,* Port Perry: privately printed by Samuel Farmer, 1934.

FILTER, REINHARD. *The Barber Dynamo: A Perspective.* The Boston Mills Press, 1977.

GUILLET, EDWIN C. *Cobourg 1798-1948.* Oshawa: Goodfellow Printing Company Limited, 1948.

HISTORICAL SOCIETY OF THOROLD. *Thorold—Its Past and Present.* Privately printed by Lincoln Graphics Limited, 1968.

JOHNSTON, AGNES ALICE. *The Late David M. Johnston, His Family and Descendants.* Port Perry: Port Perry *Star,* 1927.

MICHAEL, BETTI. *Township of Thorold 1793-1967.* Toronto: Armath Associates Limited, 1967.

NORDEGG, MARTIN, edited by T. D. Regehr. *The Possibilities of Canada Are Truly Great.* Toronto: Macmillan of Canada, 1971.

PAIN, HOWARD. *The Heritage of Upper Canadian Furniture.* Toronto: Van Nostrand Reinhold Ltd., 1978.

QUIMBY, GEORGE IRVING. *Indian Life in the Upper Great Lakes.* Chicago: The University of Chicago Press, 1960.

SCADDING, HENRY. *Toronto of Old.* Toronto: Oxford University Press, 1966.

TAIT, GEORGE. *One Dominion.* Toronto: The Ryerson Press, 1962.